I0828386

FIGHT, GRIN & SQUARELY PLAY THE GAME

THE 1945 LOYOLA NEW ORLEANS BASKETBALL CHAMPIONSHIP & LEGACY

RAMON A. VARGAS

Published by The History Press
Charleston, SC 29403
www.historypress.net

Copyright © 2013 by Ramon Antonio Vargas
All rights reserved

First published 2013

ISBN 978.1.5402.3296.0

Library of Congress CIP data applied for.

Notice: The information in this book is true and complete to the best of our knowledge. It is offered without guarantee on the part of the author or The History Press. The author and The History Press disclaim all liability in connection with the use of this book.

All rights reserved. No part of this book may be reproduced or transmitted in any form whatsoever without prior written permission from the publisher except in the case of brief quotations embodied in critical articles and reviews.

For Anna, Mom, Dad, Rosie and Danny—I love you. Your love has inspired me to achieve things I never would have thought possible for myself.

Contents

Foreword

Thanks to Ramon Antonio Vargas, *Fight, Grin and Squarely Play the Game* tells us the New Orleans Saints were not the first team to lift the spirits of their city at a time of crisis. Yes, the Saints have done it twice, both in the watery wake of Hurricane Katrina and following the worst oil spill in this country's history. But in the spring of 1945, the storybook Loyola Wolf Pack did it once as well—and once was enough.

Loyola did it as World War II was winding down, at a time when the school's alums were fighting and dying in Europe and the Pacific. They did it by bringing Louisiana its first national basketball championship as the surprising winners of the NAIB (National Association of Intercollegiate Basketball) tournament in Kansas City.

How much of an impact did a wartime basketball victory have? That's the slice of history Ramon Antonio Vargas hands to the reader. Once it happened, you had a bombardier wiring congratulations to Coach Jack Orsley from Italy. You had an alum who had shot his way through the Okinawa landing with the Marines, following the tournament over the radio and writing the coach, "You keep turning out teams like that, and the morale of our boys will go up 100 percent." These were among numerous telegrams and letters that poured in from across the country and overseas.

Vargas tells you how important the university newspaper, *The Maroon*, was at the time. Loyola servicemen, some in camps thousands of miles away from home, praying they'd be spared from being cut down by enemy bullets or mortar shells, scanned the headlines of *Maroon* issues mailed to them, and they felt slightly but crucially closer to home. He introduces you to a homegrown championship team that came out of a dilapidated, wooden structure on Freret Street that served as the Wolf Pack gym.

There was high-scoring forward Leroy Chollet, a Holy Cross School alum who could jump out of the gym. There was lockdown defender John Casteix from Jesuit High School, who did not play basketball in high school. There was freshman forward Tommy Whittaker, a member of city and state championship teams at Jesuit. There was freshman guard James "Red" Hultberg from Warren Easton High School, known for rebounding, defense and scoring. There was big Joe Gurievsky from Fortier High School. And there was Jim Bonck, a center from Jesuit who joined midway through the season and blossomed into a key piece on a historic team.

It would turn out that the Wolf Pack lost one of its top players, Sam Foreman, an outstanding perimeter marksman from Lake Charles, to the military service–related rules of the day. He would not have the chance to compete in the national tournament, which made Loyola's journey to a championship showdown against a heavily favored Pepperdine team all the more amazing.

Vargas does an excellent job of taking us back to a local 1940s sports story that had its blemishes, detailing how the championship team's star was essentially exiled from New Orleans for reasons that are unthinkable today. Perhaps fittingly, the player went on to great success while the program he left behind declined. Still, Vargas correctly maintains that the long-ago championship merits celebration. It was won by a team of heroes' heroes. And, on the basketball court in 1945, Loyola had no bigger hero than Leroy Chollet.

—Peter Finney, *Times-Picayune* sports columnist

Author's Note

Only one basketball team in the history of New Orleans has won a national championship at either the college or pro level. One. It was not Pistol Pete Maravich's New Orleans Jazz. It was not Chris Paul's New Orleans Hornets. Neither was it the University of New Orleans, Tulane University, Dillard University, Southern University at New Orleans or Xavier University.

The honor belongs exclusively to Loyola University New Orleans, a small Jesuit university founded in 1912. That will come as a surprise to almost all of the city's modern-day residents. The Wolf Pack has not competed in the top-flight National Collegiate Athletic Association since 1972, when Loyola discontinued all intercollegiate sports for nearly twenty years. Since reinstating athletics in 1991, several Loyola men and women have had distinguished careers in sports such as volleyball, basketball, baseball, cross-country and track. The women's basketball team has secured regular-season conference titles. It has won its conference's post-season tournament. It has advanced to the quarterfinals of a thirty-two-team national championship tournament.

But none of those athletes came close to bringing a national title to a city that waited until 2010 for its beloved Saints football team to win its first Super Bowl. Perhaps that is why most people are shocked that Loyola brought Louisiana its first-ever basketball championship during the spring of 1945. That team joins McNeese State's 1956 men's team, Grambling State's 1961 men's team and Louisiana Tech's women's teams in 1982 and

Loyola's campus is seen from south to north in this 1925 photo. In the forefront is "the horseshoe" and Marquette Hall, just off St. Charles Avenue. *Courtesy of Loyola University New Orleans, J. Edgar & Louise S. Monroe Library Special Collections & Archives, New Orleans, Louisiana.*

1988 as the only clubs in the state to win college national championships in basketball in either the NCAA (Louisiana Tech) or NAIA (Loyola, McNeese and Grambling).

I learned about this story in my work as a sportswriter and editor at *The Maroon*, Loyola's campus newspaper since 1923. To take a break from my usual beat, I developed a taste for writing historical features about great teams and athletes of long ago. I found decades-old issues of *The Maroon* and devoured stories chronicling the feats of Coach Jack Orsley and team stars Leroy Chollet and Jim Hultberg. The dispatches showed their age by calling Chollet, Hultberg, their teammates and opponents "cagers," which way, way back was sportswriting jargon for "basketball players."

Nonetheless, the unprecedented exploits of the 1944–45 Loyola Wolf Pack energized me. I just knew it would have a similar effect on my fellow students and graduates that had yet to discover this tale. I also knew it would have the same strong effect on people who love New Orleans sports, as I have done since I was born in suburban Jefferson Parish in 1986. Sometime at the end of my freshman year in 2006, I decided I would one day immortalize all of this in a book. I wanted to present this tale to a modern generation.

It was a complicated undertaking. There were no readily available statistics. No one from Loyola's current sports department was on staff during the era I wanted to study. Regardless, I dug up archived university records; seemingly ancient copies of *The Maroon*, which were stored in no discernible order; old daily newspapers; and twelve-inch-thick scrapbooks compiled by librarians or relatives of the athletes.

These materials chronicled the 1944–45 Wolf Pack basketball team's adventures, their triumphs and their defeats—and I found it well worth my time, because I was no longer simply a fan. I was chronicling a mostly forgotten past. I could not resist the material, and I tracked down and interviewed surviving team members and their relatives.

When I realized that many of these athletes, their relatives and friends still reside in Louisiana, I also realized how deep this historic team's local roots ran. That was the last bit of convincing I needed to see this project through. And now, it is my privilege to bring to you this tale, starring the only team from New Orleans to ever end their season on top of the basketball world—a team that then watched its best player leave for a reason no rational person today can fathom.

Acknowledgements

I owe a lifetime of gratitude to Virgin Islands journalist and filmmaker Michael Nissman, my former sports editor at *The Maroon* and one of my best friends in college. His love of obscure Loyola University history and sports history was contagious. He provided me guidance with the writing of the book. He helped research and even conduct a couple of the interviews for it while we researched a larger Loyola University sports history project that is on hold. Thank you, Michael, for all you taught me. You deserve all the best.

For the time they spent weathering my circuitous and broad line of questioning, I owe special gratitude to Jack Atchley, Ray Laborde, Jim Hultberg, Marion Hultberg, Joe Gurievsky, Sam Ciolino, David Chollet, Michael Chollet, Lauren Chollet, Robert Chollet Gordon, Byron Bonck, Scott Whittaker and Patricia Whittaker. For helping me gather records, photographs and data, thank you to the following people at Loyola University: Associate Athletic Director Brett Simpson, Athletics Director and Head Men's Basketball Coach Michael Giorlando, sports historian Felix Gaudin and Art Carpenter and Trish Nugent of the Monroe Library's Special Collection section. Matthew Hinton, thank you for your splendid photographs; Bruce Eggler, thank you for copyediting my manuscript before I turned it over to my publisher; and Peter Finney, thank you for participating in this project with your foreword.

And, of course, to The History Press and commissioning editor Christen Thompson—I will never be able to thank you enough. I was about to give up on ever publishing this book when I got in touch with Christen. Christen: when Hurricane Isaac struck the New Orleans area and I was unable to turn in to you the official proposal you asked me for, thank you for calling me, asking me if I was okay and then doing everything you did to make this book a reality.

Aside from the records and personal interviews I consulted, I compiled this narrative by researching numerous newspaper and magazine articles. The source of all material is cited in-line when appropriate, and there is a works consulted section in this volume as well. I thank the original authors for their meticulousness in chronicling one of the most fascinating sports tales I have ever encountered.

Chapter 1

A World at War Disrupts a City and a Basketball Team on the Rise

The Loyola Fight Song, original chorus lyrics

Fight! Fight! Fight! You men of the South!
We hail your courage born of old,
Fight! Fight! Fight! You men of the South!
Loyola's honor to uphold;
You men who fight and grin, and squarely play the game,
We know that you go in, a victory to claim;
So, Fight! Fight! Fight! You men of the South!
For the Old Maroon and Gold.
Make a Gold. RAH! toast! Make a boast! to Loyola's warriors bold!
Cheer again! For the men! Who defend Maroon and Gold!
So cheer them right, with all your might! RAH! RAH! RAH! RAH!

—Written by the Reverend Charles C. Chapman, S.J.; Raymond McNamara and Milo B. Williams, J.D., 1923

With his peerless passing, dribbling and scoring, freshman Sammy Trombatore forced his basketball coach at Loyola University in New Orleans to start him in the game in which the school had a chance to clinch its first-ever conference championship. Trombatore did not let his coach, John C. "Jack" Orsley, down that Monday, March 4, 1942. He hit six field goals and two free throws for fourteen crucial points against Spring Hill College, one of Loyola's fiercest rivals.

Sam Trombatore was Loyola's star basketball player in the early 1940s. Expectations were high for him in the 1944–45 season—if he would be able to play. *Courtesy of Loyola University New Orleans Athletics Hall of Fame.*

The Loyola Wolf Pack won 51–45, and thus the program earned its unprecedented Dixie Conference title. The five-foot, eleven-inch Trombatore ended up scoring as many points as Loyola's senior captain, its veteran leader, six-foot, eight-inch James J. "Big Jim" McCafferty. He was selected for all-conference honors. He was growing into a star who made winning a habit. And he was becoming a cornerstone around whom Orsley and Loyola could build a championship basketball team—or so the school and coach thought.

Before arriving at Loyola, Trombatore led his New Orleans high school, St. Aloysius, to the state championship in 1941. Then, as a college rookie, he rapidly became the second-highest scorer on a fourteen-win Wolf Pack, contributing to victories over schools such as Millsaps, Howard (now known as Samford), Spring Hill and various colleges in the state of Louisiana.

"Sam was as smooth as silk," Orsley would marvel. "He could hurt you as much with his passing and his feinting as he could with his scoring. He could fake a defensive man out of his sneakers. And he did it with the grace of a ballet dancer."

Sam Ciolino, who played basketball for Loyola in the 1940s, echoed that praise, saying, "Sam Trombatore could fake out people like you wouldn't believe. More people than you could count fell because of his fakes."

With World War II ongoing in the backdrop in the next season, Loyola and Trombatore played sixteen games against their traditional opponents, like Spring Hill, Millsaps and Howard, and they also took on teams of military servicemen stationed around the region. Trombatore led the Wolf Pack in scoring, and Orsley's team won fourteen of its games. By virtue of its excellent record, Loyola could fairly claim it was the champion of its conference a second consecutive year. "This was Loyola's best year in history," New Orleans' *Times-Picayune* newspaper declared.

Basketball officials noticed, and they invited Loyola to play in the National Association of Intercollegiate Basketball championship tournament in Kansas City in March 1943. The Wolf Pack certainly would have loved to go, especially since Loyola had never been asked to participate in the tournament.

However, of the nine players Loyola would have had available for the competition, two—starting guard Milton "Whitey" Jackson and substitute

Milton "Whitey" Jackson was a starting guard for Loyola's basketball team during the 1942–43 season, when the Wolf Pack went 14–2 and earned a national tournament invitation. *Courtesy of Loyola University New Orleans, J. Edgar & Louise S. Monroe Library Special Collections & Archives, New Orleans, Louisiana.*

guard Frank Kiernan—were called to active service with the U.S. Army Air Corps the week the university got its tournament bid. Another, starting guard Bob Segura, a reserve military officer in the dentistry school, could not leave campus due to travel restrictions for students.

That left six players whom Orsley could take to Kansas City—five on the court and one on the bench. The coach knew he did not have enough men to field a competitive squad, even with a talent like Trombatore on his side. So Orsley, also Loyola's athletic director, declined the invitation, disappointing as that was to the university's community. "The draft board was catching up with our boys," the coach explained.

When the 1943–44 season arrived, the draft board had not yet caught up with Trombatore. And because of that, he was as dominant as ever as Loyola vied for the New Orleans Senior Amateur Athletic Union title, facing teams from local recreational clubs and military facilities. In a particularly memorable 47–39 Loyola victory that year against a team representing New Orleans' Kingsley House Community Center, Trombatore erupted for thirty-six points. Of course, that means all of Kingsley House outscored Trombatore by a scant three points on that occasion.

Knowing they had a dominant basketball team, Loyola fans in the early 1940s would board chartered buses and travel to away games to cheer on the Wolf Pack. *Courtesy of Loyola University New Orleans, J. Edgar & Louise S. Monroe Library Special Collections & Archives, New Orleans, Louisiana.*

Loyola finished with a 21–3 record and won the Senior AAU league (the Wolf Pack competed there because its normal conference had suspended play due to the war). It was the first season in which Loyola's basketball team had reached twenty wins. Trombatore scored 488 points despite missing five games due to a sprained ankle. Otherwise, he would have undoubtedly tallied more than 500 points, a vast figure for a basketball player in those days. With his scoring average of 25.7 points per game, Trombatore earned a place on The Associated Press' All-America list, as well as the epithet "Point-a-Minute."

"The way Trombatore made the goals was the thing!" the *Times-Picayune* wrote that year. "He made them from the left side, from the right side and from the middle—they all looked alike to him."

The war prevented a national championship tournament from being held in 1944. However, if that tournament came back after the 1944–45 season, Trombatore's All-America credentials meant that Coach Orsley's Wolf Pack had to be considered a contender. But such lofty expectations were shattered by a terse *Times-Picayune* dispatch on April 11, 1944, that read, "Sammy Trombatore, sensational basketballer for Loyola this past season and nominee to the All-America team, is scheduled to leave today to enter the active service of the United States Army."

Trombatore, at the very least, was going to miss what would have been his fourth season at Loyola. Trombatore's departure crushed Orsley. In Orsley's opinion, Trombatore possessed more all-around ability than any other basketball player he had ever coached.

Now, there was no telling whether Trombatore would ever play basketball for Loyola again, or whether he would come back to New Orleans at all. The dream of building a championship team around Trombatore was over.

World War II, of course, didn't just disrupt Trombatore's basketball career and the Loyola Wolf Pack's ambitions. The fighting had disrupted the lives of all New Orleanians, among them Loyola students such as Luke Cuccia, a U.S. Marine Corps sergeant who was sent to fight in the Pacific.

The night before a battle against Japanese soldiers in the Philippines, Sergeant Cuccia attended Mass and received Holy Communion. At sunrise, he charged into blankets of machine gun and artillery fire unleashed by the Japanese. "On my first day up, a Japanese mortar exploded a foot from my head," he wrote in a letter addressed to the Reverend Joseph A. Butt, S.J., for whom the university's College of Business is named. "I attribute this miraculous escape to my faithful carrying of the rosary."

Cuccia's letter expressed a measure of dark humor. "Except for sniper fire and some shellings, things haven't been too bad for me," the sergeant wrote.

He also described how the marines' "ruthless" enemies would "kill civilians and burn their houses" as they retreated. Cuccia's patrolling had taken him through blazing, smoking Filipino towns. The island's natives evacuated their neighborhoods with whatever food, clothing and animals they could round up as they tried to flee the perils of the war. Cuccia recounted how the inhabitants of a land that became poorer and more desolate each day the war raged—a land far from New Orleans—were ready to give what little they possessed to American marines hailing from places they probably had never heard of.

"As [we] pass through, we see happy people again," Cuccia noted. "In this particular area, the people give us eggs, bananas and some fruit. On the way down, Filipinos throw bananas into our trucks."

While Cuccia was able to share his tales from the war, other Loyola servicemen were not fortunate enough to have that opportunity. Lieutenant Colonel John A. Butler, a 1930 Loyola graduate, spent fifteen days fighting against some of the twenty-two thousand Japanese soldiers defending the Pacific island of Iwo Jima. The fifteenth day took him to the front lines on a matter. As the eleven-year marine veteran headed back toward headquarters, a Japanese mortar shell tore through his Jeep.

The blast killed him and two other passengers and wounded the driver, according to a dispatch by Staff Sergeant Henry Giniger obtained by the university. Giniger added, "One of the most courageous and aggressive battalion commanders on the island, Col. Butler…had met and conquered some of the stiffest opposition that the Japanese offered, and all during the battle northward, the colonel had been on the front lines."

As the 1944–45 basketball season approached, Loyola University celebrated a Mass in memory of thirty university alumni who were killed in the war. A sophomore music student blew the bugle piece "Taps"—traditionally performed at American military funerals—at the consecration and at the end of the Mass. "Loyola men have given their lives to protect our way of life, therefore it is only fitting that the university should honor them with a special service," the Reverend William Crandall, S.J., dean of the College of Arts and Sciences, told *The Maroon* before the Mass.

Another priest at the university, the Reverend Loyd Hatrel, S.J., added, "It is in accord with [the] Catholic spirit that Loyola, holding dear her sons who have given their all that our way of life may prevail, solemnly and publicly pays patriotic and religious homage to her…alumni who have died in the service of this country."

Though not slain, other Loyola students suffered wounds during the war. Among them was *Maroon* sports editor Ed Fricke. After he was hurt in the fierce fighting around the Siegfried Line in Germany, Fricke wrote in a letter to a professor, "Here I am…in England, with my hand all shot up and practically nothing to do. I'm not getting any mail, and when I write, I have to write left-handed. Incidentally, my thumb is gone, and it looks really odd."

Despite his missing thumb, Fricke managed to write in his letter that the heavy fighting allowed him to see parts of France, Belgium, Luxembourg and "too much of the Siegfried Line," composed of Nazi forts and tank defenses. "We ran into some forts there that looked as big as Bobet Hall," an academic hall at Loyola that today houses the university's philosophy, foreign languages, history and English departments, Fricke wrote. "In one," he added, "we had to kill 270 Germans to take it."

One line of Fricke's missive poignantly illustrated what young men from Loyola and New Orleans faced when they left their loved ones, went overseas and charged into combat. "All my buddies are up there on the First Army front, but I guess a lot of them are gone," he wrote.

It was obvious that the Loyola community was weathering a time of loss and crisis. A Wolf Pack triumph on the basketball court would enliven and inspire its fans, its campus and its city. But, as things stood shortly before the 1944–45 season tipped off, there seemed to be little chance that Jack Orsley and his Wolves could actually do that. Besides the unavailability of Trombatore, just two key players were returning from the previous year's team. Almost everyone else was a freshman.

Chapter 2

Few Old Faces, Many New Ones

John Casteix and John Sanders "Sam" Foreman were the two main players coming back to Coach Orsley's team for the 1944–45 basketball season. Foreman, with more than two hundred points in the 1943–44 campaign, was Loyola's second-best scorer behind Trombatore, and Casteix had notched more than one hundred points—a decent showing in that era for someone at the guard position. Both lettered, both had experience and both were made co-captains by Orsley. Foreman perhaps had more maturity than anyone else Orsley would have at his disposal for 1944–45.

Before attending Loyola, Foreman had enrolled in a dentistry program offered by the U.S. Navy at Southwestern Louisiana Institute in Lafayette (now the University of Louisiana at Lafayette). He lettered in basketball and baseball prior to graduating from SLI in 1943. Foreman then opted to extend his participation in the navy's dentistry program at Loyola. He was twenty-four when the 1944–45 campaign tipped off, considerably older than his incoming teammates.

Foreman and second-year man Casteix, an alumnus of New Orleans' Jesuit High School, offered a measure of versatility to Orsley. They had reputations as tough defenders who could lock down the opposition's best scorers, yet they could also break out offensively. Foreman scored twenty-four points during his best offensive outing in the 1943–44 season, and Casteix tallied sixteen in his top showing, relatively impressive numbers for that era of basketball.

On the coaching side, Orsley could count on assistance from "Big Jim" McCafferty, hired to be Loyola's assistant athletic director months after he

Members of the 1944–45 Loyola Wolf Pack. *Bottom to top, left to right*: Sam Foreman, Johnny Casteix, Jim "Red" Hultberg, Warren Willkomm and Sam Ciolino; T.J. Whittaker, Leroy Chollet, Jack Atchley, Jim Bonck and Ray Laborde; Coach Jack Orsley, A.C. Waldrep, Assistant Coach Jim McCafferty, Joe Gurievsky and Reverend Lester Guterl. *Courtesy of Loyola University New Orleans, J. Edgar & Louise S. Monroe Library Special Collections & Archives, New Orleans, Louisiana.*

helped the school capture its first conference championship in 1942. "Between Jim McCafferty and Jack Orsley, they scouted the other teams and told us what to expect," Foreman would remember decades later. "Their coaching was superb."

Meanwhile, the new players that Orsley inherited all had credentials of various sorts. Among those shining brightest was Thomas J. Whittaker, better known as "T.J." or "Tommy," who scored well. He had helped Jesuit's basketball team win city and state championships as a senior in 1944, landing All-Louisiana honors. He played catcher and third base for Jesuit's baseball team as well, winning American Legion city, state, regional and sectional championships in 1942.

There was James "Jim" Hultberg, or "Red", who lettered in varsity basketball and baseball as a senior at New Orleans' Warren Easton High School. Thanks to the scoring ability he was bringing to the Wolf Pack, he led Easton's junior varsity basketball team to a city championship in 1942. Hultberg would jump into passing lanes, snag errant passes, tenaciously defend dribblers and relentlessly attack rebounds. It earned him the reputation of a player who was "second to none in all-around play."

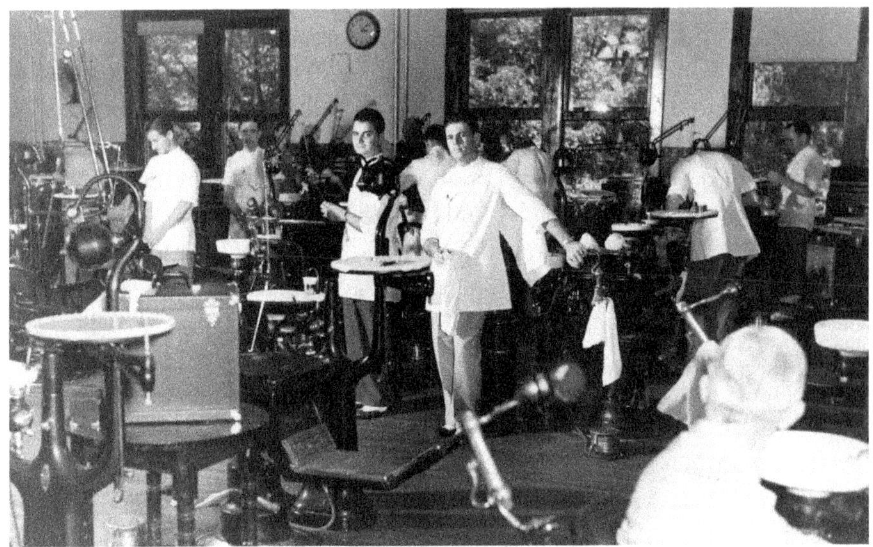

Many members of Loyola's 1944–45 basketball team studied dentistry. In this undated photo, Loyola's aspiring dentists study their field inside Bobet Hall. *Courtesy of Loyola University New Orleans, J. Edgar & Louise S. Monroe Library Special Collections & Archives, New Orleans, Louisiana.*

There was Sam Ciolino, a Jesuit graduate who said he joined the team because he had extra time on his hands as he approached the end of his dental studies. He was an All-Loyola intramural quarterback for the university's dental school junior's football team in 1944. And there was Joe Gurievsky, a product of New Orleans' Alcee Fortier High School, who was recognized as a senior All-Prep basketball center during the 1943–44 season. A year earlier, the six-foot-four, 240-pound Gurievsky made the junior All-Prep team by leading Fortier with a team high 143 points. He was a fabulous athlete who won top honors as a shot-putter for Fortier's track team and earned the bronze in a pair of discus competitions.

"Joe is young and still has plenty of time to develop," Orsley would say. "Coordination and timing gained through experience will make him a fine center."

However, if there was anyone who could fill the void left by Trombatore's departure, it was nineteen-year-old Leroy Chollet. A 1943 graduate of New Orleans' Holy Cross School, Chollet led his alma mater to three city prep-league championships, as well as back-to-back state titles his junior and senior years. In one of those state tournaments, he averaged more than sixteen points a game, tops in Louisiana in those days.

Chollet had the reputation of being a master athlete. On Holy Cross' track-and-field team, he won a prep title in the high jump, recording a leap of five feet, ten inches. As a junior, he played outfield with Holy Cross' 1942 city champion baseball team and was one of the prep league's best hitters.

Upon graduation from high school, Chollet served eleven months in the navy but was discharged due to undisclosed physical disabilities. While in the navy, he led a basketball team from an air station in Colorado in scoring. Orsley sensed that the Holy Cross product who had joined his ranks had the potential to be very special. The coach told *The Maroon*, "Chollet will possibly develop into one of the finest basketball players Loyola has ever had." A reserve on the 1944–45 team, freshman Jack Atchley from Jesuit High remembered having no doubt about that. "In that era, Leroy Chollet was as good as anybody—if not the best," Atchley said.

The Wolf Pack, who wore either white uniforms with gold trim or maroon-and-gold ones, played their home games in a gray, wooden gym on Freret Street.

The Loyola Wolf Pack played their home games in this tiny, wooden gymnasium, built in 1922. It sat on the north end of campus. *Courtesy of Loyola University New Orleans, J. Edgar & Louise S. Monroe Library Special Collections & Archives, New Orleans, Louisiana.*

Opposite: The interior of Loyola's gym wasn't spacious, and the floor was undersized, making it hard to believe the building was home to a varsity college basketball squad. *Courtesy of Loyola University New Orleans, J. Edgar & Louise S. Monroe Library Special Collections & Archives, New Orleans, Louisiana.*

Built on the north end of Loyola's campus in 1922, the gym had an undersized floor and a maximum seating capacity of only 730. Journalists politely described it as "antique" until Loyola tore the gym down in 1953 and replaced it.

It was in that tiny gym that Loyola opened its season on December 2 against a team representing a U.S. Army air field in Big Spring, Texas. Foreman was out with a minor leg injury. Orsley started reserves and quickly rang up a 6–2 lead. The coach later sent in Chollet, Whittaker, Hultberg, Casteix and Gurievsky, and they responded by building up a commanding 34–21 lead. The freshmen had to deal with some mild jitters at moments during their first game together, and at times the team's passing was sloppy and not as precise as it should have been. But there was secure defensive play from Wolf Pack reserves Atchley, Bill Browning, Fred Chaplain and A.C. Waldrep. Sam Ciolino supplied some scoring off the bench for Loyola. Leroy Chollet racked up a game-high nineteen points, and T.J. Whittaker had fifteen points. Loyola ultimately recorded a convincing 59–38 victory.

The Maroon newspaper was already describing the Loyola duo of Chollet and Whittaker as "stellar." But then the Wolf Pack clashed at home on December 8 with a team from Bergstrom Army Air Field in Austin, Texas, and events unfolded quite differently for Loyola and its supporters. The main reason for this was that Bergstrom had a couple of accomplished players—William C. Staiger was a former local Amateur Athletic Union star, and James Flanagan had played with Penn State. The duo formed part of one of the highest-scoring teams Loyola could expect to face.

Foreman was available against Bergstrom, but Orsley again started his reserves. That quintet fell behind quickly, so the coach deployed what he considered a stronger rotation: Chollet, Whittaker, Hultberg, Casteix, Foreman and Gurievsky. Loyola fought back a bit, but by halftime, Bergstrom had a 33–22 lead. Loyola tried to close the deficit with fourteen points from Foreman, twelve from Joe Gurievsky and another dozen from Leroy Chollet. In fact, the Wolf Pack outscored Bergstrom in the second half 33–28. But the efforts of Chollet, Foreman and Gurievsky fell short. Loyola lost to Bergstrom 61–55. Staiger led the visitors with eighteen points, while Flanagan had seventeen.

The loss against Bergstrom raised serious questions about Loyola's freshman-heavy squad. Could these prep standouts make it at the collegiate level? Could they cut it against service teams featuring some players who had already enjoyed illustrious careers at their respective universities? First-year players like Sam Ciolino weren't sure. Many years later, Ciolino said, "We just thought we were another basketball team."

Chapter 3

"They're Fast-Break Artists"

The Wolf Pack had another chance at Bergstrom the following day in the Loyola gym, and they weren't about to back down. This time, Loyola built a slight 28–26 lead at halftime. Though Bill Staiger dropped sixteen points on the home team, Loyola's Joe Gurievsky equaled that total with five field goals and six free throws of his own. Gurievsky had backup from Leroy Chollet and Sam Foreman, who each contributed a dozen points more. T.J. Whittaker had eight points. Loyola prevented Bergstrom from spreading out its scoring, and the story turned out to be much different from the previous game's. The Wolf Pack beat Bergstrom 54–42, avenging its earlier loss and showing it could rebound from adversity well.

If the Wolf Pack wasn't careful in its next home game on December 14 against New Orleans Naval Air Station, not even one week later, the game could easily have gotten away from them. The navy squad boasted a 1942 All-America guard, Lieutenant J.B. Renick of Oklahoma A&M, now Oklahoma State. Other players had worn the colors of larger universities such as Purdue, Georgia Tech and Baylor.

Each team defended well in the first half, and Loyola barely led at halftime 15–14. Loyola limited Renick to three field goals overall, but the All-American converted seven free throws to lead all scorers in the game with thirteen points. The problem for Renick was that the rest of his team combined to score just sixteen points. The Wolf Pack, meanwhile, got many more of its players involved on offense and spread the scoring out. Whittaker paced Loyola's offense with twelve points on five field goals and two free throws. Chollet and John Casteix each netted six points, while Foreman and Red Hultberg each had five points to help Loyola win 37–29. "In the late stages of the game, they pulled away to gain a handy victory," the *Times-Picayune* reported.

Through the first four games of the season, Leroy Chollet had been mostly quiet, leading Loyola just once in scoring. That emphatically changed in the Wolf Pack's following three games. On December 15, in the first half against Brookley Army Air Field of Mobile, Alabama, Chollet poured in twelve of Loyola's first thirty points, while the entire Brookley team could muster only thirteen. Chollet added another seven in the second half to finish with nineteen points on eight field goals and three free throws in the Wolf Pack's 65–29 shellacking of Brookley. The rest of Loyola's scoring was distributed well among the roster, as no one, aside from Chollet, had more than eight points for the Wolf Pack, which is what T.J. Whittaker amassed on four field goals. *The Maroon* lauded Chollet as "the star of a Wolf team that dominated play all the way."

Chollet went into his next performance on December 20 at home with an even hotter hand. Though Loyola fell behind 6–2 early to the local Naval Repair Base, Chollet led the Wolf Pack to a 36–30 lead by halftime. Loyola then widened its lead to twenty-three points with eight minutes left and held on for a 65–52 victory. Chollet connected on an impressive twelve field goals and seven free throws for thirty-one points, almost half of Loyola's total production on offense that day. No one from the local Naval Repair Base managed even half of that. For Loyola, T.J. Whittaker (eighteen points on nine field goals) and Red Hultberg (ten points on five field goals) also performed well.

Chollet did not ease up at the Loyola gym two days later against a U.S. Coast Guard Air Station team from Biloxi, Mississippi, about ninety miles from New Orleans. He again topped all scorers in the game with nineteen points. In fact, Chollet sank his eight field goals and three free throws in the first half of the December 22 matchup. That is because after Loyola built up an irreversible 31–12 lead at halftime, Coach Orsley sent in his second unit to finish the game out. None of Chollet's teammates reached double digits, though Hultberg and Foreman came close with nine points and seven points, respectively. The top-scoring Coast Guard player had eleven, and Loyola's staunch defense limited all of his teammates to four points or fewer.

The Coast Guard game was the Loyola basketball team's last contest before Christmas. As gifts, Loyola's fans had received a salvo of sixty-nine points in three games from Chollet and a 6–1 record to start their first season without their ex-star Trombatore. Loyola was averaging fifty-five points a game and holding their opponents to forty-one per outing, stats which in those days indicated Loyola had a strong offense complemented by a formidable defense. Of the Wolf Pack in action, it was said, "The team is geared to the offensive. They're fast-break artists and in addition employ many plays. Signals are called, and the players react just as does a well-drilled football team."

INTERLUDE: OFF THE COURT AND ON THE TOWN

The arrival of Christmas in 1944 meant the Loyola community had some free time to spend. Jack Atchley, when not playing basketball as a reserve for the Wolf Pack or just for fun, went to the Teen Canteen, established by the Key Club at the school then known as S.J. Peters High School. When it existed, the canteen was located at 700 South Jefferson Davis Parkway, right at Tulane Avenue, and it was open until 8:00 p.m. weekdays and until midnight on Saturday. The city provided the space for the canteen rent-free.

There was a jukebox and a large dance floor at the canteen. Small tables surrounded a bar stocked with soft drinks. There were tennis facilities and a variety of parlor games. "It was a place where all us young guys went to meet all those young girls," Atchley said more than six decades later. He and his teammates could only walk there—they couldn't gather the $1,600 it cost to purchase a basic, two-door car.

Other students looking to have a good time outside of the classroom did so by hitting the streets of New Orleans with a date for a fraction of what it would cost their counterparts several decades later, judging from the writings of *The Maroon*'s campus life reporter at that time, Jeannette Mumme. "Can you scrape together two bucks, buddy?" she began one of her articles. "If so, you're ready for a date tonight."

One of the spots Mumme suggested guys take their ladies to was Lenfant's, a seafood restaurant and lounge in the 5200 block of Canal Boulevard, tucked into Greenwood Cemetery. A typical night went something like this: you'd walk inside and straight ahead to the coat-check room, and if you had made one, the reservations desk. If you were going to eat, the dining room was on the right—there were dozens of tables, set with white cloths, napkins and flowers in diminutive vases. Waiters wore

This postcard shows what New Orleans' Canal Street looked like in the 1940s, when Loyola was conquering the world of small college basketball and students were looking for a fun time out on the town. *Author's collection.*

white aprons and black bow ties. If you didn't have enough money to pay the entire bill, and you were young, they'd give you an "I owe you" note, and you could settle up the next time.

However, it was the dimly lit lounge to the left of the entrance that drew Loyolans and other young New Orleanians. According to a retrospective on Lenfant's published in the *Times-Picayune* many years later, there was an enormous jukebox whose lights reflected off the parquet floor. Visitors belted out school cheers or danced to tunes like "Sentimental Journey" from Doris Day with Les Brown & His Band of Renown; "All the Things You Are," recorded by artists such as Mildred Bailey, Glenn Miller and Frank Sinatra; and the ubiquitous "I'm in the Mood for Love."

Folks drank beer, Tom Collinses and soft drinks. They ate french fries. They filled ashtrays with cigarette butts. Then, they went home before their parents got mad about how late it was.

Mumme claimed that 80 percent of university undergraduates she polled concluded that a movie downtown followed by a few numbers worth of jitterbugging to a swing band would "make a very enjoyable evening." By the time the boy dropped the girl off at the doorstep of her home, he had spent between three and five dollars.

In 1940s New Orleans, when pricey nights out were ten dollars, the Blue Room at the Roosevelt Hotel was one of the best places Loyola students—or anyone else, for that matter—could go on a date. *Author's collection.*

Theaters back then sold "admit one" passes to movies such as Fred MacMurray's *Double Indemnity*, Humphrey Bogart's *To Have and Have Not* and Rita Hayworth's *Cover Girl* for a nickel. Mae Cain, an arts and sciences senior interviewed for Mumme's column, said, "I especially like to go out…and dance; then, since it's on the way home, stop and eat. If a boy has money, I'd like to help him spend it, but if he hasn't, it makes no difference if we just dance."

That perhaps wasn't unreasonable, according to the Loyola men Mumme interviewed, as they agreed that four dollars "for a show and then dancing at the Fountain Lounge [at the Roosevelt Hotel on Baronne Street] or Lenfant's was good date material." At least one Loyola man was a big spender. Student Sal Federico told Mumme that ten dollars "is appropriate for special occasion and Blue Room dates." A delighted Mumme quipped, "Line [for dates with Federico] forms to the right, girls."

As pricey as Federico's dates at the Roosevelt's Blue Room were those days, that wouldn't pay for a single movie ticket on many nights, in many cities, in the twenty-first century, thanks to inflation.

INTERLUDE: OFF THE BATTLEFIELD

Abroad, the war forced members of the Loyola community serving in the military to seek other forms of entertainment. While on leave, some went sightseeing. Others, such as Captain Rafael Diaz, stowed away their tools or weapons and picked up songbooks.

Diaz was stationed in "merry old England," as he put it in a letter to *The Maroon*, before noting that the country wasn't "so merry anymore" after so many years of fighting. Diaz, on top of his other responsibilities at his base, belonged to a glee club that "put on lots of shows in the wards of nearby hospitals" to bring back some of the lost cheer.

Others thought of home when they went sightseeing. A letter printed in *The Maroon* and signed by Lieutenant John P. Briant as he "was enjoying the Italian sunshine" relayed, "Naples is quite a city. It brings back memories of New Orleans and the States, although it is scarred by the war. While there, we went to the Isle of Capri and saw the Castle of Tiberius and the famous Blue Grotto."

However, the price of admission to such marvels a world away from Loyola's peaceful classrooms and its Uptown New Orleans neighborhood could be steep.

Lieutenant F.L. Lombardo wrote to a Loyola professor about his sightseeing in Paris: "I could write pages describing its beauty." Instead, he spent just a couple of lines on a piece of paper and let the names of the sights speak for themselves: the Eiffel Tower; the Seine River; the Trocadero, a garden area across the Seine from the Eiffel Tower; the Arc de Triomphe; La Concorde, a public square; the Opera; Montmartre, a hill; Notre Dame Cathedral; and the Parisian catacombs. A fascinated Lombardo described the catacombs as "a huge burying place with layers of human bones and skeleton heads. There are some three million bodies in this place."

Others wrote home just to have something to do, proudly explaining the roles they played in the war effort while understandably referring to their enemies in politically insensitive terms. Lieutenant N.F. Murphy sent greetings to the university from aboard a battleship in the far Western Pacific: "Our mighty dreadnought has four invasions under her belt, and more than one Jap aviator will never again see Tokyo because of her." A Navy ensign wrote in to the university and bragged about a Loyola alum named Jack Rau, a marine first lieutenant who earned a Silver Star for gallantry as part of an artillery battalion during the Battle of Saipan and had the reputation of being "quite a Jap killer."

Meanwhile, some soldiers with Loyola ties spent time thumbing through copies of *The Maroon* or even writing to the editors of the student publication. On the pages of the paper could appear something from which to draw inspiration as the war dragged on. And seemingly no one was sure when the hellish conflict would end. Army captain Elias A. McColloster, a former *Maroon* news editor and 1942 Loyola journalism graduate, captured that despairing sentiment in a letter that was printed in his old college paper during the 1944–45 school year.

McColloster had been on the front lines of battle while making his way through Belgium, Luxembourg and France. One day, he walked through the Imperial Cathedral in Aachen, Germany. His steps echoing around him, he headed to the tomb of Charlemagne, the founder of an empire encompassing much of modern-day France and Germany. "It felt funny to be in that cathedral, looking at those men and thinking of [Charlemagne] and how it was partially his fault all of this fighting is still going," he wrote in his letter. "For it is just a hangover from his partition and his land."

Then McColloster's thoughts turned to the fighting ahead, as he remarked, "The Germans have proved that they can fight, and have men left, too."

From England, Ensign Paul W. Schott wrote in another letter reproduced in the Loyola paper: "Once in a very great while, I receive a *Maroon*, and

Loyola students of the past read a copy of the university's newspaper, *The Maroon*, which chronicled the basketball team's exploits and was mailed to school community members in the armed forces. *Courtesy of Loyola University New Orleans, J. Edgar & Louise S. Monroe Library Special Collections & Archives, New Orleans, Louisiana.*

always enjoy reading through it, and in my own mind, turning back the pages of time. The happiest days of my life were spent at Loyola."

Corporal William J. Wegmann, stationed in Waikiki, Hawaii, wrote in yet another letter that he enjoyed reading *The Maroon* "immensely." It helped him keep track of what his former classmates were up to and what the school's organizations were doing, he said.

What McColloster, Schott, Wegmann and other soldiers receiving *The Maroon* via the mail could also read about was a Loyola basketball team that had gotten off to a much better start in the 1944–45 season than anyone could have expected. Those soldiers would be able to follow the further exploits of Jack Orsley's Wolf Pack. And they would be exhilarated by them.

Chapter 4

"The Pack Appeared Certain Goners"

When it returned to action after the Christmas break on January 5, 1945, Loyola's basketball team did not get the chance to ease back into things. It faced Foster General Hospital, a team from a U.S. Army medical center in Jackson, Mississippi. After racing to a 6–0 lead, Foster General was ahead 24–17 at halftime.

Six-foot, five-inch center Jim Coven of Foster General dominated the Wolf Pack, rejecting shots, grabbing rebounds and scoring fourteen points. Leroy Chollet and T.J. Whittaker answered with some offense of their own, scoring seventeen and twelve points for Loyola, respectively.

With less than thirty seconds to play, the game was deadlocked 50–50. But the Wolf Pack's last shot did not go to either Chollet or Whittaker; it went to Joe Gurievsky. Perhaps not expecting that Gurievsky would have the ball in his hands so late in the game, Foster General left him open. Gurievsky took advantage of the oversight. He calmly positioned for a set shot, released the ball and buried it in the goal. The shot catapulted the Wolf Pack to a two-point lead.

But trouble wasn't over for Loyola. Foster quickly in-bounded the ball after Gurievsky's basket. One of the Foster players popped off a desperation shot from half-court and missed. There was a mêlée under Loyola's basket for the rebound, and Whittaker was fouled. He subsequently shot a free throw that could have ensured the victory for Loyola, but he failed to convert it.

Coven rebounded for Foster. Loyola's five defenders swarmed around him, and he couldn't get a pass off to a teammate. The whistle blew. Loyola had won, 52–50.

Having emerged on top in the tensest situation it had been in so far, the once lightly regarded Wolf Pack was making believers out of anyone who watched the team play. Chollet was the new Trombatore, the *Times-Picayune* suggested. He, Whittaker, Gurievsky and Hultberg would deal the damage to opponents offensively, while Casteix and Foreman were in charge of slowing the enemy down with their defense. "This young team will make competition interesting for all opponents…and will mold into a strong machine capable of meeting the best college teams in the country," the *Picayune* wrote.

Though the contest against Foster turned out to be as close as it could, the fact that Loyola won offered the school's fans a measure of solace. "Followers of the Pack calmed their badly jangled nerves somewhat with the thought that at least future games could be no closer," *The Maroon* reported.

How wrong they were.

On January 7, Loyola clashed at home with Gulfport Army Air Field. The Wolf Pack struggled to cope with the opponents' torrid fast breaks and led just 12–11 after the first quarter. The margin remained the same at halftime, with Loyola up 23–22 while playing at home in front of a packed house, the largest crowd of the season.

Then, with half a minute left to play in the game, Gulfport found itself ahead 50–49, ready to send Loyola's supporters to the exits in disappointment. Gulfport had limited Chollet to seven points. Whittaker fared only slightly better with nine points. Loyola's top scorers that day were Red Hultberg and Sam Foreman, who each had thirteen points as the game ended.

On the final possession, Loyola entrusted its fate to co-captain Foreman, who got the ball, dribbled to the half-court line and eyed the goal hulking over the playing surface. At a distance of forty-two feet, it was seemingly miles away. The ball must have weighed as much as a mound of cannonballs. The rim must have appeared to be the size of a thimble.

But Foreman was open, wide open. Free to shoot—the seconds ticking, ticking, ticking from the clock and the gym vibrating with nervous energy—Foreman heaved his ton of cannonballs hopefully.

A hush fell over the gym as all eyes tracked the ball's flight. Foreman's shot sailed into the goal.

The hush vanished. The stands erupted in celebration. Loyola won 51–50. The Wolf Pack had improved to 8–1 at the expense of a team composed of players who used to star at prominent basketball programs such as Ohio State, Louisiana State University, Oregon and Nevada.

More than sixty-seven years after his heroics against the Gulfport Army Air Field, Foreman said during a telephone interview that he still remembered netting his miraculous shot that January 7 in 1945. "I could see the line…I could see the goal, so I took it," he explained coolly. "It made my day, I'll promise ya that. It made my day."

Loyola next met their old Dixie Conference rival Millsaps at home on January 9. Foreman continued converting long-range field goals. T.J. Whittaker parked himself under the opponents' basket and devoted himself to connecting on layup shots from up close.

Millsaps mounted their own attacks against Loyola, but a number of their shots that appeared accurate instead smacked the rim and rolled out. "The Millsaps lads tried hard [but] couldn't get organized [and] lacked luck," the *Times-Picayune* recounted.

Millsaps' frustration became apparent. Two of their top players were whistled for too many fouls and were ejected. Meanwhile, Loyola bulled its way to a 27–14 lead at halftime and ultimately routed Millsaps 52–36.

Chollet and Hultberg recorded nine points each. Whittaker ended the game with fourteen points, and Foreman had thirteen on four field goals and five free throws. The *Picayune* singled Foreman out for his "shifty dribbling and excellent defensive play" as well. For the second game in a row, he showed how valuable his experience and maturity could be to Coach Jack Orsley. Orsley was glad to have him, especially when defenses succeeded in shutting down Chollet.

When an overflow crowd filled Loyola's gym on January 12 to watch the locals take on the Lake Charles Army Air Field and its star, ex-Columbia University All-American Billy Hasslinger, the Wolf Pack was riding an eight-game winning streak. They felt ready for Hasslinger, an Army captain, as well as his teammates.

But Hasslinger and Lake Charles were just as ready for Loyola. They kept pace with the home team and were trailing just 29–27 at halftime. Lake Charles, however, was playing with just two substitutes. As their players tired, Loyola pounced. Chollet torched Lake Charles for twenty-two points on eleven field goals, and Foreman wasn't far behind with eighteen points on nine field goals. Whittaker aided the Wolf Pack's cause by making six shots from the field for a dozen points, and Hultberg had ten points on four field goals and two free throws.

Casteix passed and rebounded well as Loyola walloped Lake Charles 73–53. Despite his team's defeat, Hasslinger did do justice to his status as an All-American by scoring nineteen points.

After the game against Lake Charles, the papers in town referred to Loyola as a "powerhouse" for the first time that season. However, the real powerhouse was the team Loyola had to face next: Keesler Army Air Field from Biloxi, Mississippi. The Wolf Pack was going to visit Keesler on the night of January 13 and then host that team in New Orleans six days later.

Keesler was undefeated. It was the defending champion of a league made up of military service teams from along the Gulf Coast. It had won twelve games in a row, and it had already beaten Tulane—Loyola's bigger next-door neighbor—and LSU, Louisiana's flagship university in Baton Rouge.

Keesler's roster included First Lieutenant Francis O'Grady, an All-American at Georgetown who had tallied nineteen points against Tulane, and Otto Kurek from Illinois, who starred in the win against LSU. Aside from those two, there was Herb Cline, All-Conference at Wake Forest, and All-American Myles Zeleznik of Pittsburgh, who had once played professionally with the so-called New York Celtics barnstorming team. "The Keesler squad…have a galaxy of ex-college stars…to throw at the Pack," *The Maroon* warned.

Loyola built an early lead against Keesler in front of 1,200 personnel at the Army Airfield, but some choice offense from Kurek and Cline put Keesler up 24–22 after the first half.

Keesler's speedy defense then clamped down on Loyola the rest of the game. A fired-up Wolf Pack defense responded by limiting O'Grady to a team-low four points for the game, but Kurek and Cline picked up the slack with eleven and ten points, respectively. Cline dominated rebounds and defending under Keesler's basket, and he passed well. Keesler pulled far ahead in the second half.

Red Hultberg countered for Loyola with five field goals and two free throws for twelve points, and Leroy Chollet recorded five field goals and a free throw for eleven points. Tommy Whittaker managed four baskets for eight points, and both he and Casteix defended well. The Wolf Pack looked like it would come back late in the game, but Keesler prevailed 42–39, snapping Loyola's nine-game winning streak and earning its thirteenth straight victory. "All told," the *Times-Picayune* bluntly commented, "the Wolves were outclassed."

Prior to the revenge match between Loyola and Keesler six days later, the service team defeated the Gulfport Naval Training Center and Eighth Naval District Headquarters to extend its unbeaten streak to fifteen games. But some felt Keesler's chances of securing a sixteenth straight win at Loyola's expense took a serious hit when Cline shipped out to the war, making him unavailable on January 19 to help out against a Wolf Pack that had lost to Keesler by only three points.

In comments he made prior to the game, Keesler coach George Huffman disagreed with the notion that his squad was vulnerable. "We know that the Loyola players left the field here with the idea of beating us when we meet them in New Orleans," he told the *Times-Picayune*. "But we've taken steps to correct the mistakes we made in beating them."

An enormous crowd packed Loyola's gym. Fifteen minutes before the game started, Orsley had to march out to the turnstiles and issue an order that no one else be let through. But things didn't go the way Loyola would have liked at first, and it seemed the Wolf Pack was going to let its giant audience down.

Guarded by A.C. Waldrep, O'Grady blasted the Wolf Pack with eight field goals in the first half. He dazzled with his shooting, dribbling, passing and defending as Keesler pounded its way to a 31–16 halftime lead in front of a shocked Loyola crowd. The Wolf Pack's aim was woeful. The locals made just four of their first thirty-seven shots from the field, a pathetic showing. "The Pack appeared certain goners," the *Times-Picayune* wrote.

Orsley sent Casteix in to replace Waldrep and try to rope O'Grady back in. Casteix responded to the occasion, and he held O'Grady to a free throw and a field goal in the second half. Then, with O'Grady in check, Keesler faltered. Otto Kurek was the only other Keesler player to amass double digits in points, with eleven.

Scoring from Chollet, Whittaker, Hultberg and Foreman steadily whittled away Loyola's deficit. Suddenly, with about seven minutes left in the game, it was just 41–39 Keesler. Hultberg knotted the score with a layup. A basket from Whittaker then nudged Loyola in front for the first time, if only briefly, as Keesler soon tied the score again.

But Chollet, Foreman, Hultberg and Whittaker buoyed Loyola to a 9–3 run to finish the match. Loyola won 52–45, ending Keesler's undefeated season and its vaunted winning streak.

Chollet accumulated five field goals and eight shots from the free-throw line for a total of eighteen points; Hultberg connected on four field goals and three free throws for eleven points; Whittaker had five field goals, for the most part on nifty one-handed shots, for ten points; and Foreman had four field goals for eight points. Aside from shutting O'Grady down, Casteix added two field goals, a free throw and five points to Loyola's victorious effort.

The Loyola crowd loudly applauded Keesler as the Biloxi crew left the court. The audience knew it had just watched one of the finest basketball teams in the southern United States in Keesler, and they knew it took the Wolf Pack every ounce of "spirited, inspired [play] to turn back" the visitors.

"The Pack couldn't pull any punches along the line," the *Times-Picayune* noted. "It was a fight from start to finish."

Loyola had bagged its most impressive win so far and simultaneously served notice that it could beat anyone it played. The city of New Orleans was clamoring to watch the Wolf Pack play, *Times-Picayune* columnist William McG. Keefe wrote. Unfortunately, Keefe observed, the compact Loyola gym's "seating capacity cannot take care of a third of the fans who would like to see the sensational Wolves in action." And, from the moment the Wolf Pack beat Keesler, tickets to Loyola's home games would be harder than ever to come by.

Orsley and his Wolf Pack traveled to Lafayette the night of January 20 to play Southwestern Louisiana Institute, Sam Foreman's alma mater. Loyola grabbed an early lead and was never threatened.

Leroy Chollet (twenty-one points) and Sam Foreman (sixteen points) combined for thirty-seven of their team's points in an easy 62-47 win, their second victory over a collegiate opponent. Foreman showed no mercy to his old school, a fact that was unsurprising to his teammates at Loyola.

"All Sam Foreman cared about was shooting that basketball," reserve Sam Ciolino would remember many years later. Ciolino, who scored two points against SLI that night, said, "Foreman got that ball, and he was going to shoot it."

Interestingly enough, in this game, future Louisiana governor Edwin Edwards' future commissioner of administration scored a point for Loyola, his only score for the Wolf Pack all season. Raymond "Ray" Laborde, an end-of-the bench guard who grew up with Edwards in Marskville, Louisiana, got it on a free throw. Loyola's reward? A January 23 home game against the Gulfport Naval Training Center, a highly skilled team whose only loss of the season had come against Francis O'Grady, Otto Kurek and the talented team from Keesler Field.

In the first half of the game between Loyola and the Gulfport NTC, neither team led by more than four—Gulfport had only a 27–24 lead at intermission. In the second half, neither led by more than a single basket. The teams chased each other from one end of the court to the other. They tussled for every pass and shot, and they challenged each dribble of the ball. Unsurprisingly, plenty of fouls were committed—the officials whistled Loyola for thirteen offenses and Gulfport for fourteen in the physical showdown.

With the score tied 46–46 in one of the game's final possessions, Red Hultberg made like Foreman and Gurievsky and nailed a clutch field goal to put Loyola up by a basket. Moments later, Gulfport's offensive leader drew a foul, advancing the ball toward Loyola's goal. But he made just one of two free throws and helplessly watched Loyola run out the last seconds of the game.

Leroy Chollet had a team-high fourteen points. Hultberg's basket got him the last of his twelve points on five field goals and two free throws, and Tommy Whittaker added nine to the victorious effort.

"From the opening tap…the two teams matched each other stride for stride," the *Times-Picayune* reported. "The Gulf Coast visitors put up a darn good battle all the way."

Things for Loyola were going as well as Jack Orsley could have reasonably hoped. The team was playing well. It was beating top-class opponents consistently. Its stars were healthy. No crisis had been able to truly test the Wolf Pack—at least not yet.

Therefore, there was no way Loyola could know how tough its January 27 matchup with a team from the New Orleans military base known as Jackson Barracks was going to be. But the Wolf Pack began sensing they were in for a fight when they quickly fell behind 6–0 at the home court of Jackson Barracks, a facility located in the 6400 block of St. Claude Avenue in the city's Lower Ninth Ward. By halftime, Loyola trailed 24–18.

The second half got physical, and things got even worse for Loyola. Chollet badly injured his back in the course of play and had to leave the contest after netting a game-high sixteen points. Then, a body block from a Jackson Barracks defender sent T.J. Whittaker into the wall of the gym, seriously hurting the Loyola player's shooting arm. Whittaker, with six points, would not finish the game either.

Nonetheless, led by Red Hultberg and his eleven points, Loyola battled Jackson Barracks to a stalemate, 43–43, as the final whistle blew. However, in the ensuing overtime, Jackson Barracks outscored Loyola 5–4, handing the Wolf Pack its third defeat of the season.

If any one loss threatened to mar the season Loyola and Orsley had been orchestrating, it was this one—a single-point, overtime heartbreaker in which the team's top scorers sustained injuries that would keep them off the court. Whittaker would have to miss at least one game, and Chollet was out for a few. Someone else from the Wolf Pack's roster would have to step up, take charge on the court and hold the team together until Chollet and Whittaker could return.

Asked during an interview in his living room six decades later if he remembered playing an especially rough team of local soldiers—one that knocked Chollet and Whittaker out of the game—Jack Atchley squirmed in his chair. Perhaps instinctively, he rubbed one of his arms (the one he would have hurt if he had been Whittaker) and answered before the end of the question. It was as if he was startled by the mere mention of a neighborhood bully from many years past—one he was thankful for not having to deal with anymore.

"Jackson Barracks," Atchley blurted. "You must mean Jackson Barracks. Oh-ho yeah, it was Jackson Barracks."

Chapter 5

Red to the Rescue

For its first game after losing Leroy Chollet and T.J. Whittaker to injuries, the Wolf Pack was able to add to its roster a player who had been discharged from the Army Air Corps in the middle of the basketball season. James "Jim" Bonck, an All-Prep basketball player for Jesuit, would help Loyola at the center position with his height of six feet, two inches. Despite a sprained hand, he debuted against the local Coast Guard basketball team on February 1 in front of yet another large crowd at the Loyola gym. However, the Coast Guard did not offer much of a test for the Wolf Pack, even without two of its best players. Loyola led 39–19 at halftime, with thirteen of those points coming from Foreman. Meanwhile, Hultberg scoured the court for steals and rebounds and shut down the Coast Guard's offensive options with impregnable defense. He also scored almost as frequently as Foreman did.

In all, Foreman had eight field goals and two free throws for eighteen points, while Hultberg finished with eight field goals for sixteen points. Reserve Fred Chaplain showed his best form of the season by notching five field goals and two free throws for a total of twelve points. Gurievsky wasn't far behind with eleven points, and Casteix had nine points. Bonck, meanwhile, sank a long field goal, tipped in a shot off the rim and, following a scramble for an offensive rebound, converted a close-range shot to tally six points. Loyola used thirteen of the players on its roster and ultimately swamped the Coast Guard 77–43. Two of the Coast Guard's players, Bob Shanks and Johnny Moore, accounted for more than half of their team's points, netting thirteen and twelve, respectively.

"The Wolves bounced back convincingly from their defeat by Jackson Barracks and really poured the pressure on…routing the Coast Guardsmen from the very beginning of the contest," the *Times-Picayune* wrote.

Loyola's next game, on February 3, probably wouldn't be such a feast. It was the return match against Jackson Barracks. A sizeable crowd flocked to Loyola's gym to see whether the Wolf Pack could capitalize on its chance for revenge. Loyola would have Whittaker back, but he was available to play only sparingly.

Loyola and Jackson Barracks played to a 7–7 stalemate a quarter of the way through the game. Jackson Barracks then seized the lead, but a flurry of successful shots from the field for Loyola resulted in an 18–10 halftime advantage for the Wolf Pack. Loyola, playing slowly and deliberately on offense due to Chollet's absence and the reduced presence of Whittaker, preserved the lead and was up 27–19 three quarters of the way through the contest. Hultberg starred for Loyola thanks to fourteen points on top of his indefatigable defense and aggressive rebounding. Foreman added eight points, while newcomer Bonck, quickly becoming a valuable member of the Wolf Pack, contributed six in his first start. Whittaker, with his arm still tender, had just three points against the team that had injured him. Nearly half of Jackson Barracks' scoring came from team leader Olavi Salminen, who had a dozen points. Loyola outscored Jackson Barracks 11–6 in the final stretch to win 38–25.

The result was most satisfying to Loyola's followers. In that week's issue of *The Maroon*, sports columnist Gernon Brown Jr. berated Jackson Barracks, boasting that Loyola didn't need the barracks' "football tactics" to win. Without becoming goons, Loyola "still gave the Jackson boys as bad a licking as good basketball permits," Brown boasted. "The Wolves still have to get around to learning these stunts, but somehow, they haven't needed them.'"

However, the void left by Leroy Chollet's injury became glaringly obvious on February 9, when Loyola clashed with the Eighth Naval District Headquarters, based in New Orleans. It did not appear Loyola was in for a struggle when they took a 15–9 lead at the start, but the Wolf Pack fell behind 27–25 by halftime. The lead seesawed the rest of the way, and Loyola found itself deadlocked 50–50 with forty seconds left to play.

Whittaker played more like himself this time, pumping in fourteen points on seven field goals. But Loyola didn't entrust its last shot of the game to Whittaker; they instead entrusted it to Red Hultberg.

Red had already amassed sixteen points, but Loyola needed him to get one more basket. Hultberg came through. As the *Times-Picayune* described it, he sank "a spectacular shot from the sidelines" and clinched the 52–50 win, Loyola's sixteenth of the year.

Following the game against the Naval Headquarters, Gernon Brown Jr. of *The Maroon* had seen all the last-minute wins by the Wolf Pack that he could tolerate. He declared in his "Sports Slants" column that "The Wolf wins have been a little too close lately; in fact, if they get any closer, the Loyola gym will have to get a good practicing heart specialist to set up shop inside its walls. He should do a thriving business."

There was no time for the Loyola players to rest, however, as they hosted Southwestern Louisiana Institute on February 10. Hoping to give his stars a few extra minutes to recuperate from the previous day, Jack Orsley sent in his second string to start the game against SLI. But the plan didn't pan out. Hungry to avenge its loss to Loyola earlier in the season, SLI bulled its way to a 12–4 lead. Orsley had to send Whittaker, Hultberg, Bonck, Casteix and Foreman into the contest before it slipped away. Loyola cut the deficit by halftime but still trailed 27–22. The *Times-Picayune* reporter covering the match observed that the Wolf Pack's fans seemed concerned that Loyola would fall to a collegiate opponent for the first time that season.

But then Hultberg restored order, knocking down three straight baskets to start the second half. Casteix then converted a free throw, and Foreman added a basket to get Loyola its first lead at 32–30. Buoyed by Casteix's aggressive rebounding and defense, Loyola preserved its slim lead the rest of the game, but the Wolf Pack struggled to expand it. The biggest lead the Wolf Pack had prior to the last four minutes was 47–44, produced by a Foreman basket. Ultimately, though, Loyola steadily expanded its lead to win 55–46. Hultberg's fifteen points on five field goals and five free throws paced Loyola. Foreman added thirteen points on six field goals and a free throw, while Bonck once again proved his value with ten points on five field goals.

Leroy Chollet at last returned to action against the local Naval Repair Base at the military team's gym in the Algiers section of New Orleans on February 13. However, he wasn't yet ready to be the player he was prior to his back injury, and Loyola again struggled for vast stretches of the game that day. The Wolf Pack and the Navy spent much of the first half tied until Loyola managed to seize a 29–25 lead at the intermission. None of those points came from Chollet. In the second half, he dribbled and passed smoothly and posted four field goals for eight points. That individual effort, though, wasn't going to get the job done for Loyola. His teammate Red Hultberg knew that and played his best game of the year. Hultberg hammered the Naval Repair Base for thirteen field goals and two free throws for twenty-eight points. He

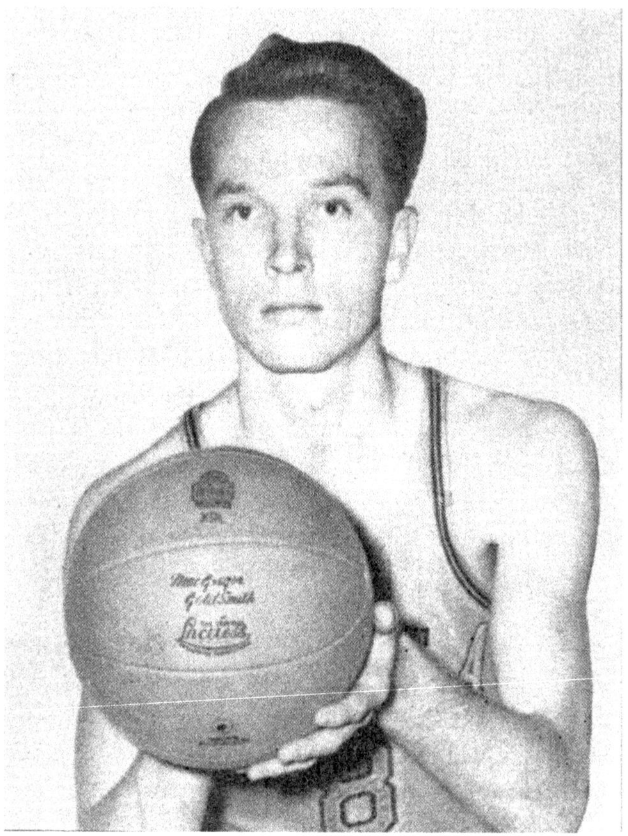

When Loyola star Leroy Chollet missed a few games due to injury, Jim Hultberg stepped up for the Wolf Pack and provided the scoring they needed to stay in championship contention. *Courtesy of Loyola University New Orleans Athletics Hall of Fame.*

complemented his offensive dominance with equally dominating rebounding and defending, boosting Loyola to a 63–52 win on the road, its eighteenth victory of the campaign. Jim Bonck had ten points, while the rest of the players who scored for Loyola tallied between four and eight points.

In the five games following Chollet's injury, Hultberg had averaged more than eighteen points an outing. As Whittaker's scoring touch cooled in the aftermath of his injury against Jackson Barracks, and Chollet's return to the court was tepid, Hultberg had reached into his past and transformed himself into a version of the player who had led Warren Easton's junior varsity team to the 1942 city championship. It wasn't so much that Hultberg was motivated by a desire to step out from the shadows of the likes of Chollet and Whittaker; it was simply his sense of obligation to do whatever it took for the Wolf Pack to triumph, said teammate Sammy Ciolino.

"Jimmy Hultberg didn't look for glory or anything," Ciolino explained decades later. "You knew that if you gave the ball to Jimmy, he was going to work hard and do what he had to do."

Loyola's ensuing two games were in Jackson, Mississippi, against Millsaps on February 16 and Foster General Hospital two days later. Facing Millsaps, the Wolf Pack trailed by as many as ten points at one time, though the New Orleanians managed to stay within striking distance. At halftime, it was 26–25 Millsaps, and in the last three minutes, Loyola engineered an offensive spurt to overtake their old Dixie Conference rivals and win 49–47. The Leroy Chollet that Loyola fans knew and loved reappeared against Millsaps. He bucketed twenty points, six of which came on three straight field goals at the end.

"Chollet…[was] back in his old form," *The Maroon* gleefully reported. Hultberg amassed ten points of his own, and Bonck had seven.

But facing Foster General, Chollet regressed. The hospital squad limited Chollet to a measly five points, and it cost Loyola badly. Foster led early with a 26–20 advantage at halftime and added twenty-five points to its total in the second half, while Loyola could manage only twenty-one points, resulting in a 51–41 loss for the Wolf Pack, the worst of the season. T.J. Whittaker had led Loyola with twelve points, and Hultberg had ten. Foster's six-foot-five-inch center Jim Coven scored fifteen points, and he and his team got even for the dramatic 52–50 loss the Wolf Pack had inflicted on them right after the Christmas break. As *The Maroon* noted ruefully, "Loyola…was a far cry off from the ability they showed earlier in the season."

"We were off on our shooting—that's the substance of it," explained Orsley, whose Wolf Pack shot poorly from the field against Foster. "The boys were way down when it came to hitting the basket."

The Wolf Pack's supporters had reason to be concerned. The timing of the loss couldn't have been worse. Orsley revealed that the National Association of Intercollegiate Basketball was on the verge of inviting the Wolf Pack to its post-season, small-college championship tournament to be held in Kansas City from March 12 to 17 that year. The bid half depended on the outcome of a February 23 game in Natchitoches—a community in Louisiana 275 miles northwest of New Orleans—between two schools the Wolf Pack never even played.

The matchup in Natchitoches was between Louisiana Normal College, now known as Northwestern State, and LSU. Henry Lee Prather, longtime coach of Louisiana Normal, was the chairman of the NAIB district Loyola played in and therefore selected the district's representative in Kansas City. Prather said he would not consider entering Louisiana Normal into the tournament unless it upset LSU. He reasoned that his team, in case it prevailed against LSU, would have beaten a much tougher collegiate opponent than any Loyola had played. If Louisiana Normal lost, however, Prather said he would favor picking Loyola because the Wolf Pack had a more impressive record and had not lost to any collegiate teams.

Fortunately for the Wolf Pack, the LSU Tigers did Loyola a favor. They beat Louisiana Normal 44–40. Now the other half of Loyola's bid depended on how the Wolf Pack fared during the final three games of the regular season. On their plate were two home games against Camp Plauche—a formidable Senior American Athletic Union team comprised of local U.S. Army soldiers who had won twenty-five of thirty-four games that season—and one against the Gulfport Naval Training Center, hungry to ruin Loyola's post-season dreams as payback for a 48–47 loss to the Wolf Pack in January.

Orsley said he intended to accept a bid to the national tournament if it was extended. Unlike what happened during the 1942–43 season, his Wolf Pack had not been decimated by call-ups to the armed services, and just one player would be unavailable for the tournament due to travel restrictions for students with military commitments. The only way Orsley's team could guarantee the invitation would be extended, though, was to earn it during the last week of their regular season.

Leroy Chollet's layups and Sam Foreman's long field goals put Loyola just barely in front of Camp Plauche on February 21. At halftime, Loyola led 25–24. But Plauche could never grab the lead from the Wolf Pack. Whenever it got close, Chollet, Foreman and Hultberg connected on timely baskets to keep Loyola on top. Foreman led Loyola with fifteen points on seven field goals and a free throw. Chollet had five field goals and four free throws for a total of fourteen points, and Hultberg hit five field goals and a free throw for eleven points. Plauche had the high scorer for the night in Hal Braden, who totaled sixteen points on six field goals and four free throws. Right behind him was teammate Bobby Richardson, who had seven field goals for fourteen points. The Wolf Pack prevailed comfortably, 60–46, for its twentieth win of the season.

When Loyola traveled to the Gulfport Naval Training Center's home floor in Mississippi on February 24, the Navy squad had lost the basketball championship for service teams to Keesler a few days earlier. The team to pay for that frustration—dearly—was Loyola. The Naval Training Center shot at the basket from all angles and hit on about 75 percent of their attempts that day. They rushed out to a commanding 38–18 lead at halftime.

Chollet, with fourteen points, and Foreman, with eleven points, fought back for Loyola. But it wasn't enough to overcome the damage done by former Iowa State University star Price Brookfield (twenty-four points) and ex-Wyoming University All-American Bill Strannigan (fourteen points), which propelled Gulfport to a 70–46 shellacking of Loyola. The rout rendered the Wolf Pack's earlier one-point win against the Naval Training Center a distant memory.

With the NAIB bid not yet secured, Loyola headed into its regular season finale against Camp Plauche on February 28. Things started off slowly, but the Wolf Pack built a 15–11 lead in the first quarter and extended that advantage to 33–26 halfway through the contest. Joe Gurievsky found himself locked in a physical, personal battle with Plauche's center, and the two exchanged fouls continuously. However, the situation didn't escalate, and Loyola held onto a 46–38 lead after the third quarter.

Loyola then punctuated its regular season with perhaps their most dominant quarter of basketball—on both ends of the court. Nailing basket after basket and snuffing out advance after advance from Camp Plauche, the Wolf Pack outscored the Plauche soldiers 27–3 in the final stretch of the game and closed out a 73–41 win, their twenty-first of the year. Tommy Whittaker drew loud applause from spectators with his eight field goals and sixteen points. Hultberg attracted nearly as much appreciation with his five field goals, two free throws and twelve points. Chollet, Gurievsky and Waldrep each had ten points in the last chance Loyola had to convince Henry Lee Prather that it deserved to travel to Kansas City for the national championship.

All told, Loyola had a record of 21–5. In twenty-six games, members of the Wolf Pack had combined for 1,419 points, an average of 54.5 points a game, while surrendering just 45 points a game. Both marks were excellent for that era of collegiate ball. For the first time ever, Loyola produced four players who bucketed more than 200 points each. Leroy Chollet racked up 132 field goals, 62 free throws and 326 points, despite missing four games. Jim Hultberg had 116 field goals, 46 free throws and 278 points. T.J. Whittaker had 112 field goals and 11 free throws for 235 points. Sam Foreman's 92 field goals and 42 free throws got him 226 points. Joe Gurievsky was the fifth and last Loyola player to crack triple digits, with 40 field goals and 31 free throws for 111 points. Loyola clearly had the weapons to compete nationally, and Prather was sold. He offered the Wolf Pack the bid, and Orsley—as promised—accepted.

As he promised he would if they were offered it, Coach Jack Orsley accepted a bid to the 1945 National Association of Intercollegiate Basketball tournament in Kansas City. He was armed with one of Loyola's best teams ever. *Courtesy of Loyola University New Orleans Athletics Hall of Fame.*

Orsley was armed "with one of the best teams ever produced by Loyola and one of the best in the South," the *Times-Picayune* wrote.

Loyola's campus rejoiced once news broke in early March that Orsley was taking the Wolf Pack to Kansas City. Everyone agreed that Loyola's run for post-season contention had been fantastic. But a national championship trophy did not seem like an immediate possibility on campus. In fact, most students' minds weren't even on basketball, though the team representing them was equipped to go deep in the national tournament. The students instead focused on developments in the war overseas, and they were split into two camps.

When the latest edition of *The Maroon* hit campus news racks shortly after Loyola agreed to go to Kansas City, the chiefs of the Allied armed forces had called for bombing raids that targeted German civilians. Many on campus, including *The Maroon*, decried the policy as "terror bombing." Others agreed with an editorial published in the now-defunct *New Orleans States* newspaper that claimed civilian bombing was tolerable "as a ruthless means of hastening Hitler's doom."

"The mass of the population shouldn't suffer for the ruthless crimes of their leaders," opined Jerome Verges, an arts and sciences sophomore. Added arts and sciences freshmen Jack Ruli and Richard Eberhardt, "Only targets whose destruction would have direct bearing on the war should be deliberately bombed. Perhaps the civilian bombing will, instead of weakening the German morale, strengthen it."

Gregory Choppin, an arts and sciences sophomore at the time, disagreed. "It's our turn to show Germany what war is really like. In the last war, Germany made peace before her country was invaded. Now, to break the morale of the people and end the war quicker, I think we should feel free to bomb them," *The Maroon* quoted him as saying.

The war, of course, steamrolled on, paying no mind to the opinions of New Orleans college students. In the meantime, Jack Orsley, Leroy Chollet and the rest of the Loyola Wolf Pack had to plan for a trip to Kansas City.

Chapter 6

A Trip to Kansas City

Jack Orsley and his team left for Kansas City on Saturday afternoon, March 10. They boarded the Panama Limited train at the Carrollton Avenue station and planned to arrive the night of March 11. The tournament would get under way on March 13; however, Loyola would not have to play its first-round opponent, Phillips University of Enid, Oklahoma, until March 15, affording the New Orleanians plenty of time to become acclimated and get in a couple of practices prior to debuting, which was preferable to having to play right away.

Players making the trip were Leroy Chollet, Tommy Whittaker, Joe Gurievsky, Red Hultberg, John Casteix, Jim Bonck, A.C. Waldrep, Sam Ciolino and Jack Atchley, the youngest member of the squad. Most were freshmen or first-year players. Another chaperon accompanying the team was the university's moderator of athletics, the Reverend Lester Guterl, S.J. The most notable absence from the tournament delegation was veteran co-captain Sam Foreman, who had made that miracle half-court shot earlier in the season against Gulfport Army Air Field. As a student in the U.S. Naval Dentistry program at Loyola, per regulations, he could not leave campus for more than forty-eight hours.

"Foreman...was our regular playmaker and a fine outside shooter," Orsley would tell a sports columnist many years later. "We were counting on him and were sick when the Navy wouldn't allow him to make the trip."

"Foreman...[was] very influential when it came to other people scoring," Atchley said. Therefore, players and fans feared Foreman's exclusion from the tournament meant that Chollet and Hultberg would be more easily bottled up. Nonetheless, the Wolf Pack felt it had one key advantage: five of its main players—Whittaker and Bonck from Jesuit, Hultberg from Warren Easton, Chollet from Holy Cross and Gurievsky from Fortier—had grown up playing with and against each other at various levels, in various leagues in New Orleans. Perhaps that is best illustrated by the fact that Chollet, Whittaker and substitute Atchley all attended the same elementary school, Sacred Heart of Jesus on Canal Street. In high school, Atchley and Whittaker competed against Chollet, as Jesuit and Holy Cross throughout history have been archrivals. At Loyola, however, they were again on the same side. "We were like a family," Atchley said decades later. "We would compete against anyone together."

In public, Orsley was confident his team could turn in a respectable performance in Kansas City. "If we play as we've done against some of the service teams this season, I believe we can go through the tournament," the coach told the *Times-Picayune* prior to departing.

But there would be challenges. Kansas City and New Orleans weren't all that unlike—notably, each city had a vibrant, legendary jazz scene, and the war had brought defense plant and armament jobs to each town. However, the unfamiliar place where the Wolf Pack would be spending much of its time in Kansas City, the Municipal Auditorium arena, could not have been more different from the small gym at Loyola.

The Municipal Auditorium arena, built in 1935, could hold up to 10,500 spectators. Its ceiling was ninety-two feet high, allowing enough space for trapeze artists to perform during circuses. At twenty-four thousand square feet, the floor was large enough and sturdy enough for elephants to walk on. The rest of the auditorium featured an array of Art Deco design elements, and its color scheme, lighting, furniture and artwork were selected to give it a lavish air. The place hosted circuses, athletic events and political conventions, as well as appearances by sitting or soon-to-be American presidents. Loyola's gym at the time was simply too cramped for any such events.

Orsley acknowledged that his freshmen might struggle under the tournament's pressure and conditions. After all, the crowds they would be playing in front of were many times larger than they were used to at Loyola or on visits to the various opponents in their region. Everything just "depends on how they react," the coach noted.

Pundits did not consider Loyola a favorite as the tournament prepared to tip off. A March 11 Associated Press dispatch surveying the field reserved that label for Pepperdine College of Los Angeles, which had lost only once to a college team that season; Eastern Washington State, which had one of the country's highest-scoring players; and Simpson College of Indianola, Iowa, which had sixteen wins and four losses.

Gurievsky remembers, "The rumor was, every time we played a game, they had [train] tickets waiting for us so we could leave for home the next day." Even so, Loyola sent out an early warning that it did not intend to return to New Orleans humiliated. Against Phillips, the Wolf Pack built a 22–10 halftime lead. In the second half, capitalizing on fast breaks and turnovers, Loyola generated another thirty-one points for a convincing 53–31 win.

Jim Bonck used the first-round matchup as an opportunity to show his gratitude to Orsley for being selected for the tournament. He topped all scorers with fifteen points. Chollet added eleven, Hultberg and Whittaker each had nine, Casteix had five and Gurievsky had four. Phillips' captain, Doran Meyers, notched fourteen in his team's fruitless effort against Loyola. He was the only Phillips player to consistently convert shots for the Oklahomans.

The Wolf Pack advanced to the quarterfinals to meet Central Normal College of Danville, Indiana, which had defeated Catawba College of Salisbury, North Carolina, 53–31 in the opening round. Some three thousand spectators were on hand for the March 15 showdown, and the crowd watched Chollet tear off twenty points on nine field goals and two free throws in a 60–46 rout. Loyola was never threatened; they were on top 31–17 at halftime. Bonck pumped in fourteen points, while Casteix hit ten. Nine points from Hultberg, four for Whittaker and Gurievsky's three rounded out the scoring.

That same night, there was a bit of drama in another game. Tournament favorite Pepperdine had to overcome an early deficit to West Texas State of Canyon, Texas, to win 52–45. "The Texans proved a surprisingly tough opponent for [Pepperdine]. The spectacular offense of the Texas five forced Pepperdine to make a fast finish," the Associated Press noted.

Loyola moved on to a March 16 semifinal matchup against Southern Illinois Normal College, which had toppled Doane College of Crete, Nebraska, 61–44. A Wolf Pack victory would earn it a berth in the National Association of Intercollegiate Basketball's Maude A. Naismith championship trophy game.

In the last moments of the semifinal, Loyola was deadlocked with Southern Illinois 35–35. The score had been tied six times throughout the game. Now the ball was in the hands of the captain, Casteix, who thus far had seven points. Casteix would try to do what his pals Sam Foreman, Joe Gurievsky and Red Hultberg had done during the regular season—bury a

John Casteix's game-winning shot in the last seconds against Southern Illinois lifted Loyola to its first-ever national title game. He will forever occupy a special place in Loyola sports history because of his heroics in the 1945 semifinal. *Courtesy of Loyola University New Orleans Athletics Hall of Fame.*

game-winning shot as time ran out. Casteix opted to spot up for a long, difficult, one-handed shot from the sideline when the opportunity to be a hero presented itself. All eyes in the stands fixated on him. He fired. Players from each team rushed to the basket and tussled for position. Loyola's men were ready to tip a miss into the goal, while Southern Illinois hoped to collect a rebound and live to fight into overtime. But the shot sailed in. There wasn't time left for anything else. Loyola won, and they were going to the national championship game.

Casteix's heroics should have inspired pandemonium, sheer ecstasy or at least considerable relief. It would have been no disgrace for the Wolf Pack to lose, as Southern Illinois had nullified Loyola's offense, permitting only Chollet to reach double-digits with twelve points. Hultberg was limited to nine points, Bonck to four and Whittaker to three. But they had not lost. They had won, and they had won dramatically—the kind of signature win many teams collect on the journey to an unforgettable title.

Nonetheless, Casteix's shot "didn't impress many people," Orsley would remark to the *Times-Picayune* in a retrospective profile published on April 2, 1989. "We had to face…Pepperdine for the championship." And Pepperdine had just routed Eastern Kentucky University of Richmond, Kentucky, 52–34 in the semifinals.

Pepperdine's players averaged six feet, four inches, as tall as Gurievsky, the Wolf Pack's tallest player—and Pepperdine had in its ranks a six-foot-seven-inch center named Nick Buzolich. Aside from being deemed too tall to be in the armed forces, in the earlier rounds of the tournament, Buzolich appeared to be on pace to break the competition's single-game scoring record of thirty-eight points, set by ex-Pepperdine player Pete Fogo in 1942. But because Fogo was serving in the army for the war and had been wounded during the invasion of France, Buzolich benched himself to preserve Fogo's mark.

In a story published in the *Ellensburg Daily Record* newspaper, Buzolich explained his decision to deny himself the record: "Fogo was a Pepperdine man, too, you know. He's over in Europe in the Army, and he's won the Purple Heart. I didn't much care about breaking his record."

Buzolich's noble gesture was as classy as it gets in elite athletics. Regardless, the Loyola players were aware that Buzolich could have broken Fogo's record if only he had wanted to.

Waiting for the championship game's tip-off time, the pressure and attention on Loyola from spectators and sports reporters mounted. John Casteix made it his mission to keep his teammates loose. Whenever he saw Pepperdine's players in the hotel's hallways and elevator, Casteix squealed, "Peppah-diyin, Peppah-diyin" in a nasally, high-pitched tone to annoy them, Jack Atchley remembers. Casteix faked slamming into doors, moaning as he collapsed to the floor in mock pain. His teammates loved him for that, for trying to keep them at ease. "He made everything seem so normal," Atchley said.

Elsewhere, Jim Bonck fretted about Pepperdine's height. He fretted so much about it that he visited Orsley to propose a strategy he implored his coach to consider trying: pressuring Pepperdine's ball handlers all over the floor for the full game, which Loyola had never even discussed during the regular season. If the Wolf Pack was going to have a chance, it had to hassle Pepperdine's players at all times, wherever they happened to be on the court, Bonck explained.

Indeed, letting someone like Buzolich run free under the basket would have been devastating for Loyola. Pepperdine would be unstoppable if it positioned itself near the goal. Loyola would have to hope for imprecise shots, but even then, Pepperdine's height advantage would permit them chances to score on second, third and even fourth opportunities from offensive rebounds. Loyola had to find a way to force Pepperdine to start taking shots as close to mid-court as possible. The height of Buzolich and his teammates would be worthless if they were shooting from fifteen to twenty feet away from the basket. A full-court press is hard to maintain an entire game, as it is so tiring, but it disrupts the opponent's offensive rhythm. A harried, bewildered Pepperdine—a quarterfinalist in the previous tournament—might find itself fumbling the ball over and surrendering fast-break baskets.

"There was no height on our ball club," a chuckling Ray Laborde would say decades later. Loyola knew it couldn't knock bodies under the basket with such tall players all game long and expect success. So Bonck's proposal made sense to Orsley, who knew his team was faster than Pepperdine. He listened to Bonck and was ready to spring a surprise on Pepperdine and the crowd at Municipal Auditorium on March 18. "Coach invited us to pick up Pepperdine all over the floor," Hultberg said. "He orchestrated the last game so we could win."

Loyola and Pepperdine fought the first half bitterly, as the lead was exchanged six times. The Wolf Pack, though, kept Pepperdine in check. It intercepted passes and scored easy baskets off fast breaks created by the mistakes its full-court pressure forced Pepperdine into. With seven minutes left in the opening half, Loyola was ahead 23–14. But Buzolich, Alden Hendrix and Ray Lawyer countered for Pepperdine, leaving the Los Angelenos trailing just 27–23 at halftime.

Then, in the second half, Leroy Chollet, Red Hultberg and John Casteix supplied the Wolf Pack's offense. "Loyola made every pass count and wouldn't shoot unless [players] had a good shot at the basket," a recap of the game in the *Times-Picayune* noted. With nine minutes to go in the game, Loyola was up 34–28. Chollet converted a two-pointer from long range, but Hendrix answered with his own basket to keep Pepperdine within six points. However, Pepperdine was unable to solve Loyola's incessant pressure, and its team soon disintegrated.

"We put the fastest men on the court and ran them to death," Gurievsky said. Ciolino added, "We stunned Pepperdine. We really messed up their passing flow. The fans couldn't believe it. Everyone thought Pepperdine would win. We were the big underdogs." Loyola racked up unchallenged baskets off numerous turnovers. Because Pepperdine had to settle for running its offense far away from the goal, Bonck turned Buzolich into a virtual non-factor. Buzolich had twelve points.

On the other hand, Chollet torched Pepperdine for eighteen points. He had five field goals and drew enough fouls from Pepperdine's defenders to hit eight free throws. Hultberg chipped in with nine points, Bonck and Casteix each had three field goals and a free throw for seven points, Whittaker and Waldrep both had three points and Gurievsky managed two points.

With five minutes left, Pepperdine coach Al Duer knew his team had been bested. He walked over to Orsley, shook the Loyola coach's hand and said he was surprised the Wolf Pack had been able to press so much. When time ran out, Loyola had triumphed, 49–36. The Wolf Pack's players leapt in the air. They embraced each other. The 4,500 people in the stands clapped and whooped, delighted that a group of first-time participants had taken the tournament. Duer marched over to the champions' locker room, congratulated them and presented them with a victory cake, Loyola's players said.

Chollet's sixty-one points in the four-game tournament earned him a spot on the First All-Tournament team and recognition as an All-American. Red Hultberg earned a spot on the Second All-Tournament team. Officials awarded each Loyola player a sparkling gold basketball with a diamond in the middle. Finally, the Wolf Pack received the Maude A. Naismith Trophy. Designed by James Naismith, the inventor of the sport of basketball, the prize was a memorial to his first wife. The trophy vaguely resembled a tall Academy Award perched on top of a base. Its legs bowed out, the figure on the prize reached both arms skyward and angled its elbows out. It held a shield from which emerged a wreath.

A distinct spot in New Orleans' sports history was forever Loyola's. Never before and never again has a pro or college basketball team from the city won a national championship—just Jack Orsley and a band of basketball players, who for the most part were groomed at New Orleans prep schools and happened to don the maroon and gold of Loyola.

"We were the first and only," Atchley proudly declared years later. Those who had believed the Wolf Pack's toughest contests would come against service teams were proved right. That year, the Wolf Pack didn't lose to a single college team.

Because the trip to Kansas City was governed by a tight budget, the Wolf Pack couldn't spend even one extra night lingering around the town it had conquered, celebrating in restaurants or bars. "Everything was pretty much set up so we could leave as soon as possible," Atchley recounted. "Yeah, there was celebrating on the trains, but it was mostly guy stuff." The national champs spent their night on top of the world wrestling and playing pranks on each other in the train's aisles. But back in New Orleans, things were unsurprisingly—and most deservedly—different. The impending placement of the Naismith Trophy in a Loyola University display case reverberated throughout the campus, the city and both theaters of World War II.

In the March 19, 1945 edition of the *Times-Picayune*, Loyola's triumph led the sports page. The "national intercollegiate championship basketball team will arrive at the Carrollton station…tonight at 9 o'clock," the newspaper told New Orleans. More than one hundred supporters packed the train station for the team's return. There were pleasant, fresh winds that night, and the temperature was a mild 70 degrees or so. It was weather fit for the kings of the small-college basketball world.

Loud howls and thunderous applause greeted the players as they stepped off the train. "They had a mob there," Gurievsky said. "All our parents, all our friends and students from Loyola, and friends from elsewhere…. It was overwhelming." Among those reveling in the Wolf Pack's honor were the Reverend Percy Roy, Loyola University's president; the dean of the school's arts and sciences college, the Reverend William Crandall; and assistant coach Jim McCafferty. Sam Foreman, barred from playing in Kansas City because of the V-12 program's restrictions, also welcomed his teammates home.

"I wish I could've gone," Foreman admitted then. Many years later, he would elaborate, "It killed me to not go—I worked so hard for it. But I have no regrets because we won it, and I am happy."

Players hugged relatives and kissed their girlfriends. Waiting for Orsley were his wife and their eight-year-old daughter, Patricia Ann. The coach kissed Mrs. Orsley and then took a moment to tell a reporter, "Victory was in the hands of everyone that played. They played a great game…and had a unified purpose. Complete team work did the trick."

Orsley's wife exclaimed, "It's wonderful." Patricia Ann declared, "I'm mighty proud of my daddy." Chollet, for his part, told the press he was just "glad to be back." He declined to discuss his own performance and instead remarked, "Jim [Bonck] was on everybody. Whittaker played his best game away from home." Meanwhile, Orsley's fellow chaperon, the Reverend Guterl, boasted that Loyola "could've beat any team in the country the way they played. Coach Orsley deserves plenty of credit. He…changed our whole system in that last game. He…ran [Pepperdine] off their feet."

Approached by a reporter, Bonck passed up the chance to clarify that he had conceived the idea of relentlessly pressuring Pepperdine's ball handlers all game long. Bonck simply said, "Coach outsmarted them." Casting a nod toward Chollet, he rhetorically asked, "How d'ya like our All-American?"

When time came to break up the revelry at the train station, Sam Ciolino led an entourage of fans to student hotspot Lenfant's. *Maroon* sports editor Emile Comar, in the mood to blow off some steam after coordinating coverage through the Wolf Pack's long but glorious season, took a crew of friends to lunch.

Meanwhile, the *Kansas City Star* newspaper raved about the show Loyola put on for Midwest sports fans:

> *It will not be far from accurate to refer to the New Orleans boys as the surprise champions. Few…gave them a championship tumble...not even after they had fought their way into the finals against Pepperdine. The Loyolans could hit the basket from any angle when they were in the bucketing mood, but it was when the enemy had the ball under the Loyola basket or in the immediate vicinity that the New Orleans boys really got down to leveling. They were tough defensively. The Pepperdines could seldom get set for a shot. Always they had to hurry, and hurried shots do not often connect.*

Maroon columnist Gernon Brown lauded Jack Orsley in his post-championship column:

> *Mr. Orsley has performed, in converting a group of New Orleans prep athletes into champs, the finest coaching job in the history of Loyola. Other college coaches have endless sources from which to draw basketball players. Orsley was restricted to locals…. Certainly the quality of basketball players graduating from high school here can't be much better than anywhere else in the country. Why, then, can Loyola afford to depend on local cagers? The answer is that Loyola has one of the finest coaches in the country.*

Times-Picayune columnist William McG. Keefe echoed those sentiments. He praised Orsley for taking a group largely made up of "freshmen from many different local high schools, graduates of many styles of play, and… molding them into a unit." Keefe continued, "Orsley was not sure just how his freshmen would perform away from home under fire, especially since the…

experienced…Sam Foreman had to be left behind. But Orsley reshuffled his team and got the best out of the boys in spite of losing one of his mainstays." Keefe then compared Orsley to Adolph Rupp, who began coaching at the University of Kentucky in 1930 and won four NCAA championships before retiring in 1972. Orsley was a "thorough fundamentalist, teaching the art of ball-handling and pivoting and footwork" to his champions at Loyola. Keefe concluded, "The fact that just [Chollet] was picked on an all-star team proves the Wolves play as a unit."

The biggest party held on the first weekend of April was in the Loyola basketball team's honor. The Blue Key fraternity threw the Wolf Pack a dance in the Loyola gym. Basketball decorations and plaques bearing the players' names adorned the scene. Student songstresses, a young man *The Maroon* called "Loyola's own Frank Sinatra" and big-band swing music heralded New Orleans' first-ever national champions. At the end of the event, Sam Foreman introduced his teammates to the crowd, who cheered them wildly. The university then held a banquet at the La Louisiane restaurant in the 700 block of Iberville Street in the French Quarter on April 9. During his remarks, Loyola president Roy hailed the Wolf Pack's work as a team. "Without cooperation with the coach and with one another, the basketball team would never have won the national championship," Roy said. Alumni Association president Joe Abraham then congratulated the basketball team on behalf of all Loyola graduates dispersed throughout the world. The team presented the Naismith Trophy to Roy.

Foreman and Casteix spoke and thanked Orsley. They cut yet another victory cake. Big Jim McCafferty called up all the members of the squad individually and gave them each a photograph of the team.

Also on hand at the restaurant were Guterl, Crandall and other Loyola deans, plus several prep school coaches. They were joined by the city's most influential sportswriters and editors.

Fred Digby of the *New Orleans Item* said the Wolf Pack's run in Kansas City "marked the beginning of great basketball in the South. [Loyola] set the pace for all Southern teams." Henry Martinez of the *New Orleans States* added, "When I saw Loyola win over Keesler Field and Gulfport, two of the strongest teams of the South, I knew that they were a club destined for a successful year."

Orsley read excerpts from the congratulatory letters that had poured into Loyola after the Wolf Pack upset Pepperdine. Pepperdine coach Al Duer wrote from Los Angeles, "I am confident that you won from the best team to represent us. I've been trying for two weeks to think of a good alibi, but the only one I can find is 'too much Loyola.' Please relay my congratulations to the boys, and may they enjoy to the full their fine accomplishments." Orsley would write back that he planned to again take Loyola to the finals soon.

There were also letters and communiqués from servicemen throughout the country and across the Atlantic and Pacific Oceans. Those letters illustrate how treasured the Wolf Pack's win was to members of the military who had attended or were attending Loyola when they were drawn into the war and their lives were disrupted. One letter was sent by Milton "Whitey" Jackson, a bombardier for the U.S. Army in Italy and a former Loyola player who was denied a chance to go to a national tournament in 1943 because of his military duty. Jackson took a break from his missions and wired to his ex-coach: "Congratulations to you and your champions. Gosh but that was swell news to me—have followed your every game via clippings sent to me by my family."

Howard Taylor, a marine stationed in California after shooting his way through the Okinawa landing, hardly waited for the championship game to conclude before firing off a letter to Orsley. Taylor enjoyed a privilege many of his fellow Loyolans in the war didn't. He followed the tournament in Kansas City over the radio. "About three minutes ago," his letter began, "I learned the Loyola University of the South won the National Intercollegiate championship. I just want to express my congratulations to you and your team. I'm just as happy about it as they are. The radio broadcast came over fairly well, and although I didn't recognize any of the boys, I was pulling for them."

Taylor concluded by summing up the season's recurring theme, the team's enduring legacy: "Well, Coach. Until I come back to Loyola, you keep turning out teams like that, and the morale of our boys out here will go up 100 percent."

Major James Thomas Conner, former dean of the law school, wrote, "Heartiest congratulations on your success. When I read the clippings enclosed in Mom's letter, I was bowled over."

Orsley read some of those letters during the Blue Key banquet. "These letters give testimony of morale building the team did," the coach told the audience in the gym.

The letters Orsley recited touched Atchley, who has never forgotten how rewarding they were for him. He said, "It made you feel good. It was nice that they were getting word as to what was going on in the city among people they were familiar with. It made us feel good that they appreciated what we were able to accomplish."

Ciolino explained, "Back then, the news of the day was the war. Then, this team came along—us—and people in town had something different to look at."

This banner commemorating Loyola's national basketball championship in 1945 hangs at the school's University Sports Complex on Freret Street. *Photo by Matthew Hinton.*

Foreman, for his part, said, "I used to read the excerpts of people writing us from overseas. And I must say, we were really proud of that."

To soldiers with ties to the Loyola community, whose world was scarred by bombshells, machine gun fire and killing, word of the Wolf Pack's accomplishments brought a singular moment of lightness and joy. Then, on May 8, 1945, the Allied Forces accepted Nazi Germany's unconditional surrender. Three months later, the United States dropped atomic bombs on Hiroshima and Nagasaki. Japan subsequently surrendered. World War II was over. The Allies rejoiced.

That monumental military victory was achieved by armed forces full of men like Loyola students John P. Briant, Rafael Diaz, Elias McColloster, Jack Rau, Luke Cuccia, Paul Schott and others. The generation those men helped form has widely been described as America's greatest. They helped to defeat Nazi Germany, Imperial Japan and its allies. They saved the world.

The 1944–45 Loyola Wolf Pack basketball team's brief moment of glory was decidedly modest by comparison. Still, that inimitable team managed to claim the city of New Orleans' only national basketball trophy. It set a school record for total wins with twenty-five—a record that still stands after six decades. It beat every team Loyola faced that year at least once, a rare feat.

And several of New Orleans' World War II veterans confessed in personal letters that the Wolf Pack cheered their hearts, boosted their hopes and excited their imaginations. To those heroes, Jack Orsley's men had become heroes themselves, for like soldiers, those men had fought, they had grinned, they had squarely played the game—and they had won.

Chapter 7

"Being Run Out of Town"

When Loyola's best basketball team in history finished the 1944–45 season, Leroy Chollet had emerged as its best player by far. He rang up a lavish total of 326 points during the regular season, despite missing four games due to injury. At Loyola's first-ever national championship tournament, he poured in another 61 points in four games—a performance that fueled the Naismith Trophy's trip from Kansas City to Loyola's campus and landed Chollet on both the All-Tournament team and All-American list.

Chollet finished seventy-three points ahead of Loyola's second-highest scorer in 1944–45. He should have been the centerpiece of Loyola basketball teams until he graduated from the school three years later as one of its greatest athletes ever—but that didn't happen. It didn't even come close to happening. Chollet never played another game for Loyola after the championship. He transferred to Canisius College in Buffalo, New York, and he became one of the best players in the history of the basketball program there. Why did Loyola and New Orleans allow an athletic treasure like Chollet to leave? Why didn't the city or the school fight to keep him on the Wolf Pack?

The answer dates back to at least 1873. That year, Leroy Chollet's paternal grandmother, Olivia Olinde, was born to a black mother and a white father. When she was about twenty-one, in 1894, Olinde had a son with Charles Chollet, a white, Swiss-born man and school principal who lived in New Roads, Louisiana, according to Michael Chollet of St. Louis, a distant relative of Leroy who has mapped out a thorough

Leroy Chollet was the best player on Loyola's championship basketball team. But Chollet never played another game for Loyola after the championship due to reasons that are unthinkable today. *Courtesy of Loyola University New Orleans Athletics Hall of Fame.*

genealogy on the family. Besides their first son, Michael, Olivia and Charles Chollet had two more boys: Alfred, in 1896, and Charles, in 1898.

It is unlikely that Olivia and Charles ever married or were even able to live together legally, Michael Chollet says. Indeed, various statutes in Louisiana essentially forbade interracial marriage and cohabitation from 1724 to 1967, when laws prohibiting interracial marriage were negated by the United States Supreme Court's decision in the landmark civil rights case *Loving vs. Virginia.*

Nonetheless, the middle son of Olivia and Charles Chollet, Alfred, grew up and married a woman named Olga Gossett. They had three sons—Robert Alfred (born 1921), Leroy Patrick (1924) and Hillary Anthony

(1926)—all of whom were one-eighth black. Those boys would grow up at 3112 Cleveland Avenue in New Orleans. They would bring athletic glory to the schools they attended, and they would not have any problems—as long as the details of their mixed ancestry were kept quiet.

When the Chollet boys were in high school and college in the 1940s, New Orleans was a segregated city. Whites and people of color were not supposed to eat together, go to school together or play sports with or against each other. Even the best college athletes were not exempt from this reality.

Star football running back Lou Montgomery, Boston College's first African American athlete, led his team to a 10–0 record in the 1940–41 regular season. Boston College earned a berth to that season's edition of New Orleans' Sugar Bowl against Tennessee. But officials prevented Montgomery from playing because he was black. He could not practice with or stay at the same hotel as the Boston College team. He nonetheless traveled to New Orleans and to the Sugar Bowl, and just to gain entry into the stadium, he had to agree to track statistics for broadcasters as a spotter. Montgomery could only watch from the press box as his Boston College teammates played in the biggest game of their lives and defeated Tennessee 19–13 on New Year's Day.

It wasn't until January 1956 that the Sugar Bowl finally allowed a black player to compete in its annual game, when Bobby Grier of Pittsburgh took to the field with his team and faced Georgia Tech. Georgia's segregationist governor, Marvin Griffin, had urged Tech to skip the Sugar Bowl rather than share the field with Grier. "The South stands at Armageddon," Griffin wrote in a telegram asking Georgia's state university system to prohibit teams from competing against integrated opponents. "The battle is joined. We cannot make the slightest concession to the enemy in this dark and lamentable hour of struggle."

Griffin eased up on his stance after an intense public backlash, and when Grier was in town prior to the game, he did get to attend some team functions. However, he was still barred from attending other gatherings with his team because they were held at segregated venues.

Pittsburgh lost the game, 7–0. Georgia Tech's sole touchdown came following a controversial pass interference call that moved the ball from the thirty-three yard line to the one. The pass interference whistle was blown on Grier.

In 1942, the year after Lou Montgomery had to watch the Sugar Bowl from the press box because he was black, the Chollet brothers—Robert Alfred, Leroy and Hillary—led the Tigers of Holy Cross School to Louisiana's prep basketball championship tournament in Baton Rouge. Holy Cross had never won the state title. But with Leroy and Robert Alfred handling the scoring and Hillary distributing the ball around with intelligent passing, Holy Cross plowed through its opponents. The Tigers beat Byrd 56–14 in the quarterfinals; Ouachita, 53–24 in the semifinals; and Istrouma, 61–45, for the crown.

Leroy netted thirteen points against Byrd, twenty-one against Ouachita and fifteen against Istrouma, an average of 16.3 points per game. Robert Alfred, nicknamed "Al," started off with five points in the quarterfinals, added sixteen in the semifinal and erupted for twenty-seven in the championship, an average of 16 points an outing. "Stars may come and stars may go, but it'll be a long time before state basketball tournament fans forget the sensational…performance of the point-getting Chollet brothers," the *Times-Picayune* recounted. "The lads were the talk of Baton Rouge, for seldom does a team rip through the cream of the state's competition with such ease."

The following year, in 1943, Leroy and Al helped Holy Cross again qualify for the state prep meet in Baton Rouge. They didn't need any assistance to advance, but they ended up getting a heap of it anyway, as the Tigers

Holy Cross School's campus at 4950 Dauphine Street in New Orleans' Lower Ninth Ward was where Leroy Chollet and his brothers were prep school basketball stars. *Photo by Infrogmation.*

drew a bye in the first round and then won by forfeit in the quarterfinals. They thoroughly routed Istrouma 42–16 in the semifinals, setting up a championship showdown with Baton Rouge High School.

Leroy tallied fourteen points on five field goals and four free throws. Al soared through the air the entire game for numerous rebounds and found time to make three field goals and a free throw for seven points. Holy Cross cruised to a 39–24 win. The Tigers clinched state championship number two in as many years, and both Leroy and Al Chollet landed on the All-Tournament team. "In neither of [Holy Cross'] two games was the issue ever in doubt," the *Times-Picayune* noted. "Istrouma was completely and hopelessly outclassed in the semifinals. Baton Rouge was much better, but the New Orleans lads rose to the issue admirably."

In 1944, while his older brother Leroy was in his first semester at Loyola, Hillary Chollet entered his last football game at Holy Cross as an All-Prep, All-State and All-Southern halfback. Hillary, broad shouldered and piston legged, had scored eighty-nine points on fourteen touchdowns and five extra points, the second-highest point total in the state. He carried the ball for an average of almost ten yards each time it was handed to him. His team lost the state title that year; however, Holy Cross subsequently had the opportunity to win the still-prestigious Catholic Youth Organization cup in a game against Francis T. Nicholls High School, their public school rivals from just across New Orleans' Industrial Canal. In front of eighteen thousand fans packing the horseshoe-shaped structure in City Park now known as Tad Gormley Stadium, Chollet scored two touchdowns in a 46–0 victory. Although the most valuable player trophy was awarded to a teammate, Holy Cross received an invaluable contribution from Hillary Chollet against Nicholls.

To follow that up, on the day Leroy Chollet left for the 1945 NAIB tournament in Kansas City with Loyola, Hillary Chollet and Holy Cross played their eternal rival, Jesuit, for the state basketball championship in Baton Rouge. Chollet and the Tigers fell behind 8–3 early before taking a 20–14 lead at halftime. Then, in the second half, Holy Cross increased its advantage, and a demoralized Jesuit failed to respond. Chollet collected a game-best seventeen points on six field goals and five free throws as Holy Cross upended Jesuit 41–24. Officials named Chollet, who led the tournament in overall scoring, to the All-State team.

Track season was next for Hillary Chollet, and he won gold in the broad jump event at the state meet. The six-foot-two, 185-pound phenom graduated as the most coveted prep football recruit in Louisiana. LSU, Tulane, Oklahoma, Oklahoma A&M, Alabama, Baylor and Duke were among a dozen schools who sought him. Aside from his sterling prep resume, he had a military draft certification of "4F," for undisclosed reasons. That meant he was not qualified for the armed forces and would have an uninterrupted college career, making him all the more valuable for the nation's heavyweight football programs.

By early July, it became apparent that Chollet was going to enroll at LSU. In its offensive backfield, LSU already had halfback Ray Coates, a Jesuit alum who would go on to play for the New York Giants in the NFL, as well as quarterback Y.A. Tittle, who would eventually play for the Baltimore Colts, the San Francisco 49ers and the Giants. Complementing Coates's and Tittle's talents with Chollet's had to fire up LSU's football-crazed fans. On top of that, Chollet would bring his championship-caliber abilities to the LSU basketball team.

But LSU was in store for a disappointing, infuriating surprise. On July 11, Chollet marched onto Tulane's campus and enrolled in the college of arts and sciences' premedical course. The next day, he started his classes. He began preparing for a ten-game schedule with the Green Wave that included showdowns with first-rate opponents such as Notre Dame, Georgia Tech, Mississippi State…and LSU. Analyzing the situation, *Times-Picayune* columnist William McG. Keefe observed, "LSU thought Chollet had made up his mind to become a Tiger. But there is lots of rivalry these days among the squad of recruiting representatives, and somebody from Tulane made a good sales talk and clamped Chollet…just when [LSU] felt sure of him."

This was too much for some people to handle. After Chollet's college choice became public, someone started spreading rumors that LSU did not want the Holy Cross star at that school anyway because he was part black. Immediately, the Chollets found themselves shunned socially. They felt unwelcome at their church. According to Mark Bernstein's book *Football: The Ivy League Origins of an American Obsession*, "Tulane quietly suggested that Chollet might find it difficult to go there." Indeed, Tulane would not admit black students for another nineteen years. A Tulane booster who knew Chollet wanted to study medicine recommended Cornell University in Ithaca, New York. So Hillary Chollet left New Orleans—his hometown and the place he had lived his whole life—and enrolled at Cornell.

Meanwhile, right around the same time, Leroy Chollet withdrew from Loyola permanently. Loyola for decades has maintained that academic troubles led Chollet to leave the school where he had done so much to win the city's first national basketball championship. In 2007, a university official said Leroy Chollet's academic record showed he did not achieve the minimum grade point average he needed to stay at the school. Much later in his life, Leroy Chollet would tell his son David, a well-known high school basketball coach in Cleveland, Ohio, that a Loyola administrator actually discovered that the basketball star had cheated on an English paper. Leroy Chollet would tell that story whenever he was exhorting his son to perform honest schoolwork and stay dedicated to his studies. "They kicked my father out," David Chollet said. "He always said he regretted it."

But there is no denying that Leroy Chollet's mysterious exit from Loyola suspiciously coincided with his brother Hillary's departure. And the explanation that Leroy Chollet had to leave Loyola because he was a bad student rings hollow. Academics are rarely a make-or-break issue for exceptional collegiate athletes. Through the years, there has been plenty of evidence of that at all sorts of schools.

Leroy Chollet joined the U.S. Coast Guard following his freshman season at Loyola. In 1946, he enrolled at Canisius College, a Jesuit school in Buffalo, New York, which was only 150 miles or so away from where his brother was studying in Ithaca. The rest of the family moved to upstate New York as well, as Bernstein noted in his book. The weather was going to be much harsher and colder there, especially in the winters, and the area was much less metropolitan than New Orleans. But there was perhaps less of a chance that people there would know or care about the Chollets' ancestry, for black athletes in the North were allowed to compete with and against whites by then.

Depending on which account one reads, the reasons why Leroy Chollet supposedly left his championship-winning team vary substantially. In at least one version, he transferred to Canisius for two reasons: he had liked Buffalo when he visited it with Hillary one time, and the program in New York was stronger—though it has never won a national title. In another telling, a Canisius coach he met in the Coast Guard successfully recruited him to the school in Buffalo.

Surveying various New Orleans newspapers from the 1940s, it does not appear that sportswriters ever reported precisely why the Chollets left New Orleans. If they did, they did not do so widely, and they certainly did not do so prominently. But Jack Atchley, Sam Ciolino, Joe Gurievsky, Jim Bonck's son, Loyola University officials not wishing to be named and Leroy's niece agree that the Chollets were exiled from town because a Chollet ancestor was black.

"It made me sad," Joe Gurievsky said in 2012. "It hurts me to think about that even today. It hurt the team because [Leroy] was a big part of the team. I was sorry he never came back. He was a great ballplayer."

Sam Ciolino, in an interview in 2012, added, "My opinion was the family left because you would get shut out of a lot of things if you were black. Today's a different environment altogether, but back then, it wasn't." Seated in the lobby of his dentist's office during the interview, Ciolino let his voice trail off, and he cast his eyes to the ground. But then, he raised the volume of his voice and continued, "I guarantee you the guys at Loyola didn't want him to leave. Leroy was the best-liked guy on our team. He had a beautiful smile. He was so well-liked."

Byron Bonck, who would talk to his dad, Jim Bonck, about Leroy Chollet from time to time, echoed some of Ciolino's sentiments: "The guys didn't care about all of that. They loved Leroy." But individually, and even collectively, in 1945, there was nothing Leroy Chollet's teammates could do to get him to stay at Loyola without the school or the city standing behind them—and neither did. Loyola would not admit an African American student until 1952, and that was to the law school. Undergraduate day programs at Loyola weren't integrated until 1962, and there wouldn't be a black scholarship athlete there until 1967. Meanwhile, blacks in New Orleans were not allowed to eat in certain restaurants, attend public schools with whites or sit where they pleased on buses and streetcars until the 1960s.

"What could we do?" Jack Atchley asked in 2007 during a conversation at his house about Loyola's national championship and Chollet's subsequent departure. His body trembled in rage, and his eyes welled in frustration before he said, "We were just regular people."

* * *

At Cornell, Hillary Chollet stood out as a running back, kick returner and safety on the football team. He missed his junior year in 1947 because of an injury, so he was given permission to play in 1949. That year and 1948 were his best years for Cornell's football team. In each season, Cornell finished 8–1 and claimed the unofficial Ivy League championship. Chollet contributed five touchdowns and four interceptions in 1948 and seven touchdowns and four interceptions in 1949. His play in 1949 earned him an All-American selection, as well as All-Ivy League and All-Region recognition.

Chollet also stood out on the basketball team. He set a single-game record for Cornell by scoring 37 points in a 70–58 loss to Syracuse on February 23, 1949, and he set a national collegiate record by hitting nineteen of twenty-one free throws that game. Cornell's best year in basketball with Chollet was 1947–48,

This page: At Cornell University, Hillary Chollet stood out as a running back, kick returner and safety on the football team. He was drafted into the NFL. *Courtesy of Cornell University Athletics.*

when the school finished 16–9. That season, the New Orleanian averaged a respectable 12.7 points a game, the second-best on his squad.

The National Football League's Los Angeles Rams—coached, coincidentally, by Clark Shaughnessy, a football coach at Loyola in New Orleans in the 1920s and 1930s—drafted Hillary Chollet in 1949. Chollet went on to become a doctor and settle in the Los Angeles area, later founding a chain of cancer treatment clinics. He had two sons and two daughters from his first marriage. After his first wife passed away, he remarried and had four more daughters, one of whom was adopted. Hillary was eventually diagnosed with amyotrophic lateral sclerosis, commonly known as Lou Gehrig's disease. Forever remarkable, instead

This page: Hillary Chollet also stood out on Cornell's basketball team. He set a single-season game record for Cornell by scoring thirty-seven points in a 1949 game. *Courtesy of Cornell University Athletics.*

of surrendering to ALS when he stopped being able to type with his hands, he learned to use a word processor with his toes, according to *Football: The Ivy League Origins of an American Obsession*. Hillary died on Christmas Eve 1989.

Meanwhile, in Buffalo, Leroy Chollet averaged fourteen points a game in three seasons. Dubbed the "Bayou Beauty," he blossomed into an All-American forward, becoming the first player there to score more than one thousand points in his career. He helped Canisius reach as high as the number-six ranking in the country despite opposing some of the nation's finest basketball programs.

Chollet's name resurfaced in New Orleans papers when Canisius faced the undefeated LSU Tigers on December 22, 1946, in Buffalo. He netted thirteen points as Canisius grabbed a 30–22 lead at halftime that night, and he finished with a game-high twenty-one points as his team stunned LSU 59–50. It was LSU's first loss to a college team since the previous season, when the Tigers had dropped a game to Kentucky, their only loss of that campaign.

Chollet, however, wasn't done torturing his ex–home state's basketball fans. LSU and Canisius again played each other in Buffalo on December 14, 1947. Chollet was forced out of the game early that day with a twisted ankle when one of his feet went through the newly installed basketball floor. Chollet had only three points on a field goal and a free throw at the time of his injury, but he returned and added seventeen points on five more field goals and seven more free throws in the last twenty minutes of the game. Canisius toppled the Tigers 52–44.

Chollet was eventually recognized as one of Canisius' all-time best players. The school inducted him into its Hall of Fame in 1964. "He was a great player to coach," former Canisius coach Joe Niland would say. "He came out every day to play, and he played as hard as he could. He was a great team player."

The Syracuse Nationals, one of the NBA's first franchises, drafted Chollet in 1949. He reportedly signed for a $1,200 bonus and a $3,800 contract. Chollet scored 157 points in forty-nine games as a rookie. He was a reserve guard, whose job was to distribute the ball and try to score only if he was left unguarded. The stars of that team were Dolph Schayes, Alex Hannum, George Ratkovicz, Billy Gabor and player-coach Al Cervi.

In the playoffs that season, the Nationals defeated the Philadelphia Warriors and the New York Knicks to advance to the final, best-of-seven series against the Minnesota Lakers, led by NBA Hall of Famer George Mikan, considered one of the league's fifty best players ever. The Nationals were tied 66–66 with the Lakers late in the first game and had the ball with about fifteen seconds to play. Cervi drove to the basket and went for a layup that would have won the game, but Mikan rushed up from the foul line and blocked the shot.

The Lakers then pushed the ball up the floor, and one of their players buried a game-clinching shot from half-court. "We were stunned," Leroy Chollet told a newspaper reporter many years later. "Cervi blamed [Nationals center] Ed Peterson. I started yelling at Cervi, 'Ed didn't lose the game—you lost the game. You cost us money.'" Syracuse did not recover, losing the series in six games.

Despite the appearance in the finals, playing for Buffalo native Cervi was frustrating for Chollet. Cervi—who, to be fair, did coach the Nationals to a title in 1955—didn't give Chollet much playing time. The New Orleanian felt he deserved more and constantly bothered Cervi about it. "One game," Chollet would remember years later in an interview with a newspaper reporter, "he got so fed up with me he said, 'You coach the team.'"

Cervi, when naming the five starters each game, apparently would always name the first four players and then pause in hesitation. Because he would always start himself, Cervi would conclude his announcement of the starting lineup by quickly saying, "aaand Cervi," and immediately running onto the court. When Chollet coached the team for a night, he imitated Cervi, naming four players as starters before rounding out the lineup with, "aaand Chollet."

The Nationals actually won the road game Chollet coached. And, to insult Cervi, Chollet sent the player-coach into the game in the last thirty seconds—which is when Cervi would usually let Chollet check in. Cervi kept his word and permitted Leroy to coach for a night, but the New Orleanian still wasn't satisfied. According to a November 25, 1968 feature in *Sports Illustrated* about Alex Hannum that mentioned Chollet's feud with Cervi, Leroy stormed into Al's room later that night and barked that he was going to beat the player-coach up and throw him out of the window. Al tensed and appeared ready to fight it out with Leroy, but he allowed some of the other Nationals to separate them. Hannum told *Sports Illustrated* writer Frank Deford, "Al knew that if he lost, Leroy was going to toss him out the window."

Chollet's second season with the Nationals was less eventful, as a right ankle injury sidelined him for all but fourteen games. He scored just twenty-four points that campaign, a total he was capable of posting in a single game on any given day at Loyola or Canisius. Chollet left the Nationals following that season. He signed with an American Basketball League team from Elmira, New York, but it folded after just one year. Chollet opted to not sign elsewhere and retired. His pro basketball career was over. Reflecting on his accomplishments later, Chollet seemed glad he had gone on his pro basketball adventure, in spite of his disagreements with Cervi. "There's good memories of playing and being associated with some of those guys," he said.

Chollet spent the summers after his pro seasons completing his political science degree. He also opened a hot dog stand in Buffalo at the intersection of Main Street and Delavan Avenue, according to information from Canisius College.

Chollet married Barbara Knaus, who was from Lakewood, Ohio. While visiting her relatives in Lakewood, he learned that a new high school, St. Edward, was being built there. According to the *Cleveland Plain Dealer*, the unemployed ex-basketballer took a job as a construction worker on the project. After the school was completed in 1951, St. Edward hired Chollet to teach civics and economics. School administrators then assigned him as an assistant coach for the basketball, baseball and football teams. Chollet became the head basketball coach from 1956 to 1960. He kept coaching and teaching until he retired in 1985.

From 1960 to 1980, Chollet served as an administrator, umpire and coach for adult and youth basketball and softball programs of the Lakewood Recreation Department. He donated money in political campaigns to several Republican candidates and tended bar at Kluck's Restaurant on West 117th Street in Lakewood. He regaled patrons with stories about playing pro ball, coaching high school ball and being one of the best basketball players ever at two separate schools. Casual patrons found the stories "hard to swallow," according to the *Plain Dealer*. But Kluck's regulars soaked them up because although "they seemed a little tall," they were true.

Loyola inducted Leroy Chollet into its Athletics Hall of Fame in 1993. That is the only time Jack Atchley remembers Leroy Chollet returning to New Orleans after his transfer to Canisius.

In the meantime, Al Chollet quit sports after he left Holy Cross. He got married to Mary Claire Sonnier, and the couple had a son, Robert, on February 27, 1945. Al Chollet served in the U.S. Navy briefly and was discharged in May 1945, according to his son. As their son remembers it, when he was about five, Al and Mary Claire split up, and the father ended up living in Buffalo. Mary Claire and her son settled in Morristown, New Jersey, where she married a man with the last name Gordon. Her son ended up taking the name Robert Chollet Gordon, and in 1979 he moved back to the New Orleans area, where he retired as a special education paraprofessional at Hazel Park–Hilda Knoff Elementary School in the suburban community of River Ridge.

In Buffalo, Leroy Chollet introduced Robert Gordon's father to a woman named Beatrice Corry. Al Chollet married Corry about 1952, according to their only daughter, Lauren Chollet, who was born some two years later in Buffalo. The family moved to Miami before Lauren was in school, and Al Chollet got a job at a post office, from which he eventually retired.

Unlike Leroy's son, Al's daughter remembers her dad was openly "resentful about what he called 'being run out of town.'"

"That's what he used to say," Lauren Chollet said. "They were run out."

Lauren Chollet says she heard rumors about crosses being burned in front of the family home in New Orleans. She couldn't verify that, but she could verify that her father drank heavily when she was growing up, and she blamed it on his past in New Orleans. Lauren Chollet recalls how her mother would argue with her dad and repeat to him, "You need to get over this. You need to get over this." Beatrice Corry would urge her husband to return to New Orleans and do whatever he could to come to terms with what occurred, but he always refused. The place had been "too unfair, racist and awful" to him and his folks.

"It traumatized him," Lauren said. "It was horrific. It changed his whole life."

In 1976, Lauren Chollet's first son was born. She said she kept her maiden name to honor her family's struggle in New Orleans. So she made "Chollet" the last name of her first-born, Frank, and she did the same for her second son, Dominick.

Al Chollet quit abusing alcohol after Frank was born. Frank grew up to play both guard and middle linebacker for the prep football team at Hollywood Christian School north of Miami. He also played baseball there. Al, proud that his grandson was keeping the Chollet athletic tradition alive, attended every game and kept track of all of Frank's statistics. At his job, Al Chollet earned a reputation for never missing work. He was given a trophy in recognition of that, an accolade he was always very proud of, his daughter recalled.

Al Chollet suffered from Alzheimer's disease in his later years. He died on June 11, 1996, at age seventy-four. Beatrice Chollet, eighty-six, died on February 8, 2004.

One of the most vivid memories Lauren Chollet has is of a time when she, her dad and her uncle Leroy—a "compassionate, loving soul and an unbelievable friend to have in life"—were together. They were sharing drinks, reflecting on their lives, and Al and Leroy told each other a number of times, "The Chollet brothers...we made it through. We made it through."

Lauren Chollet said, "The Chollet brothers did make it through. Considering the circumstances, they did a phenomenal job."

Chapter 8

Dentists, Teachers, Coaches and Politicians

Many of Loyola's wartime basketball players grew up to become dentists, educators and coaches in New Orleans and Louisiana. A couple of them ventured into politics, and one had a particularly noteworthy career in the Pelican State's government.

Coach Jack Orsley once told a columnist, "More important [than the national title is the fact that] many of the athletes went on to make contributions in the community."

Most members of the 1944–45 Loyola Wolf Pack have since passed away. When this book was completed in 2013, Jack Atchley, Sam Ciolino, Sam Foreman, Joe Gurievsky and Jim Hultberg were alive, as well as Ray Laborde and Frank France, two reserves who became notable community figures.

Following are brief sketches tracking the lives of some of Loyola's basketball players and coaches from the 1940s before and after the capture of the Naismith Trophy, as well as a recap of the Loyola basketball program's history since then.

Samuel "Sammy" Trombatore

Sammy Trombatore returned to Loyola and played basketball there again in the 1946–47 and 1947–48 seasons following his service in the war as a sergeant with the U.S. Army's 86th Infantry Division. The Wolf Pack performed respectably

After returning to Loyola in 1946, Sam Trombatore rejoined the basketball team and led the Wolf Pack to memorable triumphs against LSU and Georgetown. *Courtesy of Loyola University New Orleans, J. Edgar & Louise S. Monroe Library Special Collections & Archives, New Orleans, Louisiana.*

in those campaigns, finishing 16–9 and 21–9. Trombatore and the team bagged a few notable triumphs in that stretch, particularly two victories against LSU and one against Georgetown.

If asked, Trombatore would say he owed his superior dribbling and passing skills to the coach under whom he won the 1941 prep state title at St. Aloysius, Brother Ralph McGarry, S.C. "There were times during recess when [Brother Ralph] would have us practicing passing and dribbling in the school basement," Trombatore told *Times-Picayune* sportswriter Peter Finney in 1984. "You played for him, and you could throw every kind of pass."

For his status as a Loyola freshman sensation, Trombatore credited his teammate, Johnny Altobello, who would later win a dozen Louisiana basketball and baseball championships coaching New Orleans high schools St. Aloysius and De La Salle. Trombatore said his teammate was "a coach on the court."

He remembers Altobello as not just an assertive teammate but also a compassionate player. Once, in practice, Loyola was shooting at a goal next to a practice basket. On one play, a defender grazed Trombatore's arm as he shot the ball, and it went into the wrong basket. An embarrassed Trombatore said to Finney, "I could have crawled in a hole. Johnny came over and told me to forget it. Told me not to worry. He really settled me down."

Trombatore eventually left the sport and worked as a salesman for Al Delahoussaye Insurance. He joked that he was also "a non-paid employee at The Plant Shop on West Esplanade Avenue in Metairie," where his boss was his wife, Edna, who owned the business.

Loyola inducted Trombatore into its Athletics Hall of Fame in 1967. The American Italian Renaissance Foundation Museum's Sports Hall of Fame on South Peters Street in downtown New Orleans later enshrined him as well. A plaque bearing Trombatore's likeness hangs near those of other distinguished Italian-American sports figures. His image keeps company with World Series–winning baseball managers such as Tommy Lasorda and Joe Torre, world heavyweight champions such as "Raging Bull" Jake LaMotta and former Loyola University baseball slugger Henry "Zeke" Bonura, who excelled in the Major Leagues for seven seasons.

Trombatore died in 1991 from cancer at the age of sixty-seven and was buried at Metairie Cemetery. Aside from his wife, Trombatore's survivors included a son and two daughters.

JIM "RED" HULTBERG

Before earning second-team All-America honors and averaging twelve points per game for the 1945 national champions, Red Hultberg was a two-sport star at Warren Easton High School, located in the 3000 block of Canal Street in New Orleans. On Easton's junior varsity basketball team, which he powered to a city championship, he honed the scoring talents he brought to the Wolf Pack—and with which he saved the championship run during a stretch when top scorers Leroy Chollet and Tommy Whittaker were sidelined by injuries. During his senior year in high school, he lettered in varsity basketball and baseball.

His whole life, Hultberg said basketball is a sport in which you do five things: score, dribble, pass, rebound and defend. While his scoring played third fiddle to that of Chollet and Whittaker in the early part of the 1944–45 season at Loyola, Hultberg excelled in the sport's four other facets. He jumped into passing lanes, snagged errant passes, pestered dribblers and chased rebounds relentlessly. It made him an enjoyable player to watch and an easy one to cheer for. *The Maroon*'s sports desk lauded him as "second to none in all-around play." Orsley would tell the campus newspaper, "Hultberg has probably developed faster and improved more than any other member of the team."

Hultberg enjoyed an uninterrupted four-year career at Loyola, for which he earned induction into the university's Athletics Hall of Fame in 1997. Once Chollet transferred out of Loyola, the mantle of stardom fell on Hultberg's shoulders. But the university never again paired him with someone of Chollet's caliber.

Hultberg still led the Wolf Pack to the national tournament semifinals in 1946, when it lost to the same Southern Illinois team it beat in 1945. Hultberg and the Wolf Pack subsequently suffered one of their worst defeats under Orsley when Pepperdine—whom they beat soundly in the 1945 championship game—walloped them 82–55 in that tournament's consolation game.

Hultberg's 11.4 points a game led Loyola in scoring in 1945–46. The main reason the Wolf Pack didn't repeat as champions, he feels, was Chollet's absence. "We never defended our title again once he left," he said during a 2007 interview.

Though his name is prominent in the story of the 1945 title, Hultberg says his favorite college memory has nothing to do with basketball. It happened before he attended his first class—way before he ever tried a layup in practice. Red Hultberg met his wife of more than sixty years in Loyola's administrative building, Marquette Hall, on registration day during his freshman year in 1944. "Once she set her eyes on me, it was over," he remembered, smiling. "I had no chance."

"What he had was no money," Marion Hultberg joked. "If we were going anywhere, we walked there." And to visit Marion, Red would walk from his house in the Lakeview neighborhood of New Orleans to her home on Fairfield Court in Metairie, about four miles away. That left little time for anything else, since his pre-dentistry workload was crushing. To spend more time around her beau, Marion joined the cheerleading team during the 1944–45 season. Just to see Red a little longer each day, she solicited and led rallying cries on the sidelines and baselines from the Wolf Pack faithful, who cheered their team all the way to a national championship.

"It was heaven watching him out there," Mrs. Hultberg said fondly. "Heaven. It was the ride of my life, that season." The cute cheerleader and her ginger-haired, light-eyed basketball star married five years after the national championship season.

Basketball was a gene that ran in the Hultberg family, and Jim's son, Jordy, inherited it. In the late 1970s, Red's kid was a two-year captain for Coach Dale Brown's LSU Tigers. Jordy Hultberg amassed two Southeastern

Opposite: After Loyola, Jim "Red" Hultberg became a dentist. With his wife, Marion, he had two daughters and one son, Jordy, a famous basketball star at LSU. *Photos by Matthew Hinton.*

Conference titles and two NCAA tournament appearances in his tenure there. Later, for several seasons, he was an on-screen personality for Cox Sports Television's coverage of the New Orleans Hornets, hosting pre-game, halftime and post-game shows as well as reporting on the city's pro basketball franchise from the sidelines. He also hosts a radio show in Baton Rouge.

Red Hultberg used to battle his son on a basketball goal in the backyard of their family home. "I knew the day was coming when [Jordy] was going to whip me," he said. "So when he was younger, I had to get my fill." Hultberg dished out defeat after defeat to his future Tiger star. But during breaks, according to Marion Hultberg, Red passed on all the advice that he could to "his baby" about the five things one does in basketball. However, there were key differences between father and son, if you ask the dad. "Jordy was a lefty," the right-handed Red Hultberg said. "And he was much better than me."

Aside from Jordy, Marion and James raised two daughters, Jan and Joanne. Mrs. Hultberg passed away on September 15, 2012, at age eighty-five. Hultberg, a retired dentist residing in River Ridge, regularly meets a group of friends for breakfast at a McDonald's restaurant on Veterans Boulevard in Metairie. "This is where we solve all the world's problems before we're done with breakfast and go on about our day doing less important things," he said in an interview.

John Sanders "Sam" Foreman

Sam Foreman married his wife, Lorraine, about six months after the national championship. He graduated from Loyola in 1946 and then served in the military as a dentist until he was discharged in 1948. While stationed in Tokyo, he started and coached a basketball team at the base. After returning from Japan, Sam and Lorraine Foreman raised a family in Lafayette. They had three sons and two daughters, and Foreman opened a dental practice that operated for sixty-three years. Lorraine Foreman died on June 8, 2012.

Foreman spent much of his adulthood playing competitive golf. He won a number of club championships and registered twelve career holes-in-one. Foreman attributed his athleticism to growing up poor on a farm during the Great Depression. He walked miles to and from school, and when he was at home, he didn't rest much—he labored on the family farm. "It sure made me tough," Foreman once told Louisiana writer Bruce Brown. "I found out I was an athlete in junior high."

Jim Bonck

There are three names inscribed on Jim Bonck's tombstone: "June," his wife of forty-eight years; "Byron," their only son; and "Loyola," where he won the title of a lifetime and prepared for his career as an educator, which he treasured.

"That was my dad," recalled Byron Bonck, a lawyer in Metairie. "Those were the most important things to him." It never surprised Byron that his father convinced Orsley to deploy the high-pressure scheme that helped Loyola prevail over Pepperdine. The son remembers his dad as "a cerebral player who understood the game, was a student of the game. He was a fundamentalist of the basic principles of the game his whole life. It would kill him if a guy drove left and shot with his right."

But basketball wasn't the only sport in which former Jesuit Blue Jay Bonck won top honors prior to college. He played on Jesuit's 1943 state championship football team. And, representing the New Orleans Athletic Club, he punched his way to the Southern AAU 175-pound novice-class boxing title in 1943, scoring a first-round knockout in the final bout. After Loyola, Jim Bonck landed work as an elementary school teacher in the Orleans Parish school system. "It was interesting because at the time, there weren't many male teachers," his son noted. "He always loved teaching."

Bonck, who had a master's degree in education, was hired as principal at McDonogh 15 elementary school in the French Quarter, where he remained for two decades or so. Byron himself was a student at that school from 1962 to 1967, or second to seventh grades, while his father was in charge. And there, in 1958, Jim Bonck almost made it into the movies. The Elvis Presley flick *King Creole* was filming at the McDonogh 15 campus, and the filmmakers asked Jim to be in the movie "because he was a big, good-looking guy," his son said. Jim Bonck indeed got to meet the King and do a bit of acting for the cameras. Unfortunately for him, that had to suffice. Laughing heartily, Byron Bonck explains, "I think they cut him out! I don't recall seeing him!"

After retiring, Jim and June Bonck moved from their longtime home in the French Quarter to Waveland, Mississippi. Jim had a heart attack while exercising and died in 2000 at the age of seventy-seven. Eleven years later, his wife died of cancer, leaving behind, among many others, Byron; their daughter-in-law, Marty; and two grandchildren.

Joe Gurievsky

Joe Gurievsky's 120 points in the 1944–45 campaign were fifth-best on the Wolf Pack, but the lore surrounding Gurievsky began even before he set foot on Loyola's campus. He became one of New Orleans' brightest prep track stars during his senior year at Alcee Fortier High School, his first season ever competing in the sport. According to a feature in the March 16, 1945 issue of *The Maroon*, he snagged three first-place awards in the shot put that year.

Impressed by his six-foot-four, 240-pound frame, the Fortier track team asked him to compete in discus throwing and the shot put in the Public High School Athletic League tournament. Gurievsky responded by winning three gold medals in the shot put and two more bronze ones in the discus, adding to his reputation as a top athlete in the Crescent City.

Gurievsky made the 1943–44 New Orleans Senior All-Prep basketball team as a center. He had been named to the Junior All-Prep team the year before by leading the Fortier Tarpons with a team-high 143 points.

When he got to Loyola, Gurievsky became the university's first second-string basketball player to score more than one hundred points in a season.

Above and opposite: After Loyola, Joe Gurievsky ran J&G Furniture Store at 801 North Claiborne Avenue in New Orleans from 1950 until about 1985. He and his wife had four children. *Photos by Matthew Hinton.*

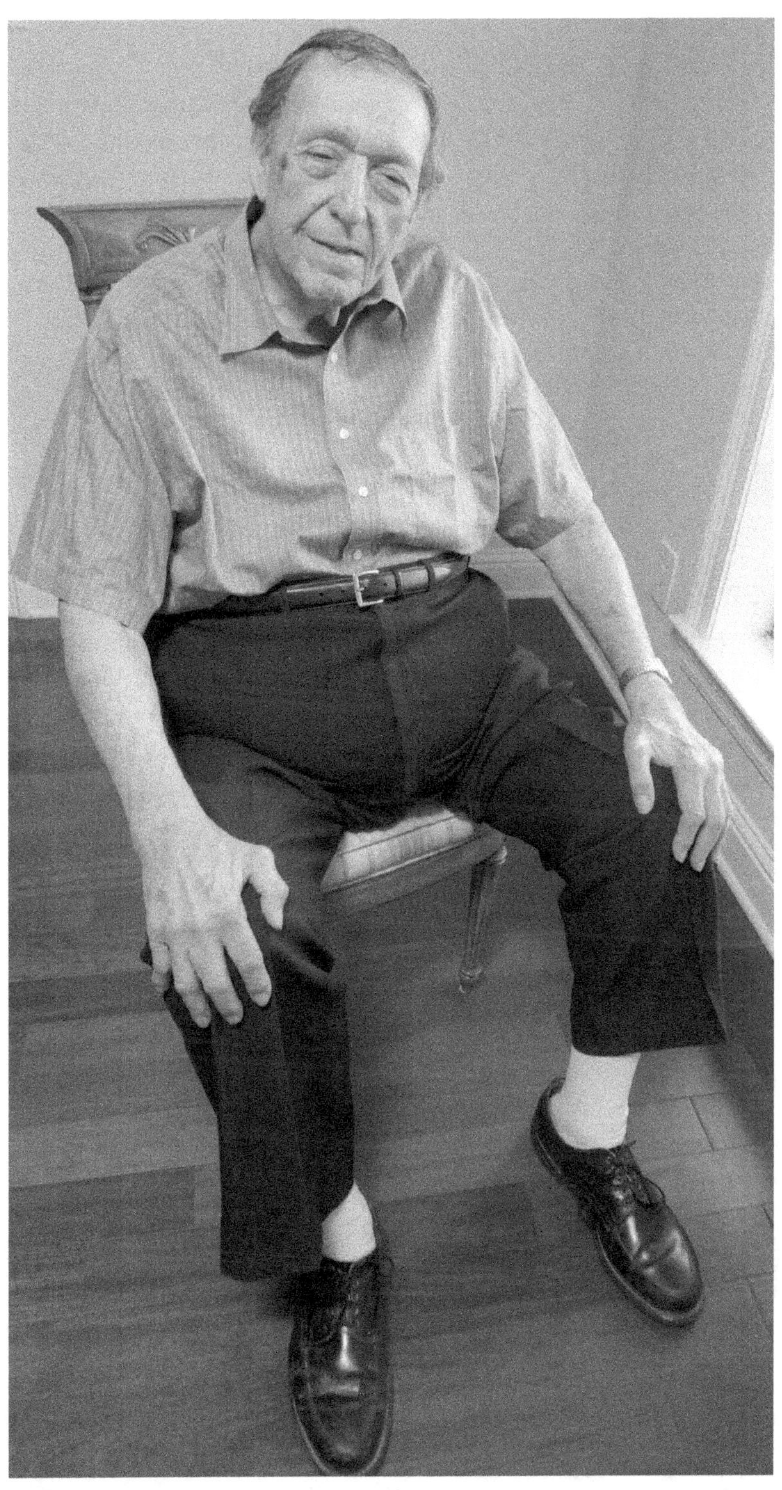

"At six-foot-four, he was our tallest guy then," Hultberg said, incredulous. "Nowadays, he'd be...too short to be even a point guard on some teams."

Gurievsky served two years in the Army Air Force after leaving Loyola. He established J&G Furniture Store at 801 North Claiborne Avenue in 1950 and ran it until about 1985. He then worked in real estate until he retired. Gurievsky married his wife, Beryl, in 1950. The couple had four children—a daughter, Evelynn, and three sons: Mark, Barry and David, all of whom played basketball as well, their dad said. Hultberg, until he retired, was Gurievsky's dentist.

"Jim was a very fine dentist," Gurievsky said. "He's always been a gentleman to me."

FREDERICK "FRED" LOUIS CHAPLAIN SR.

Frederick "Fred" Louis Chaplain Sr., a graduate of St. Aloysius High School, served in the U.S. Navy during World War II. He left Loyola and attended Southwestern Louisiana Institute, from which he subsequently matriculated.

Chaplain worked as a pharmaceutical representative for Wyeth Laboratories prior to retiring. He married Martha Bardwell in 1950, and together they had four sons and four daughters. The Chaplain boys were Frederick Jr., Daniel, Patrick and David; the girls were Margaret, Victoria, Peggy and Linda. Chaplain died of cancer on August 16, 1994. He was seventy years old. He rests at Greenwood Cemetery.

JOHN "JACK" ATCHLEY

The whites of Jack Atchley's eyes grew red whenever he spoke about the fallout from Leroy Chollet's departure. His jowls vibrated in frustration. His hazel eyes welled with tears as the feeling of helplessness he felt in 1945 when the family of his elementary school friend was forced to leave town again overcame him. Meanwhile, his wife, Elise, corrected him under her breath on memories, anecdotes and facts that have since slipped his mind.

Opposite: Once he left Loyola and served in the U.S. Navy, Jack Atchley developed a passion for horseshoe pitching. With his wife, he hosted competitive horseshoe-pitching leagues in his backyard in Harahan. *Photos by Matthew Hinton.*

On the other hand, Atchley's eyes lit up during a 2007 interview when he talked about enlisting in the navy after Loyola. He remembered how filthy he was on the train ride to the base, rolling through the countryside with the windows down, mud caked onto his skin. "You wouldn't believe it," said Atchley, who enlisted after the national championship. "It felt so good when we got to the base and finally got cleaned off."

While in the navy, Atchley remembered, he played in the backfield for a service football team. He once scrimmaged against a team of collegiate all-stars from Mexico City. In front of a large crowd, Atchley remembered, the quarterback misfired a pass, striking the New Orleanian in the back. As it rolled off his back, Atchley cradled the ball with one of his arms stretched backward. The fans screamed, "Olé!"

"It was like I was some superstar," Atchley said, guffawing. "'Olé! Olé!' They must have thought I was really good, but that was probably my only catch like that ever."

Atchley worked for a garage door manufacturer for three decades prior to his retirement in 1993. In his free time, he found a passion for, of all things, horseshoe pitching. Atchley became the commissioner and founder of a horseshoe-pitching league in his backyard in Harahan and assisted in the formation of the Louisiana State Horseshoe Pitchers Association in 1982.

Elise Atchley, who boasts that she is a better pitcher than her husband, has won numerous local and state championships, and she even landed one world-class championship. The Atchleys, parents of four children, are both inductees of the Louisiana Horseshoe Pitchers Association Hall of Fame. Jack Atchley's eyes and complexion enliven when discussing the percentages of the best horseshoe pitchers in the state, region, nation and even the world. It is the exact opposite of his demeanor when discussing what happened to the Chollets after Kansas City.

When visitors to his home one day peppered him with questions about the 1944–45 Loyola basketball team, Atchley was eager to fish around in his memory for stories about a group that he was "so proud to be a part of." He could quickly name his teammates, describing each of them affectionately as "a great man," "a very, very nice guy" and "out of this world."

JOHN CASTEIX

Every championship basketball team needs a player like John Casteix on its roster, Red Hultberg said. "Casteix was always [guarding] the best players and played very well against them."

Like any good captain, Casteix led with a calm poise, especially when the stakes were the highest. That was never more apparent than when Casteix hit the game-winning shot in the last seconds of Loyola's 37–35 victory in the national championship semifinals against Southern Illinois—a shot that lifted the Wolf Pack through to the finals and its unique place in New Orleans sports history.

Casteix played five seasons for Loyola, until 1948. He achieved a master's degree in education and later became a teacher and sports coach at Eleanor McMain Junior High School. He was also president of the New Orleans Coaches Association.

In 1966, Casteix made news by running for state representative of New Orleans' Seventh Ward. He promised to support legislation promoting responsible government and the continued industrialization of the state. He also called for repealing an act that kept the price of milk artificially high for consumers, expanding educational and residential facilities for children with special needs and setting a more realistic salary schedule for police, firefighters, public school personnel and other state employees. He wanted to invest idle funds better, reallocate existing taxes to prevent future tax increases and enhance state support for flood control in the hurricane-prone New Orleans area. However, when the primary election occurred, Casteix failed to make the runoff.

Casteix was married to Lucille Lussa Casteix. Together, they had four children and resided in the 6000 block of Elysian Fields Avenue in New Orleans. Casteix died in February 1983 at the age of fifty-five. Loyola inducted him into its Athletics Hall of Fame in 2011. His citation lauded his specialty as a defender, his game-winning goal against Southern Illinois and his status as the team's co-captain, alongside Foreman.

ALFRED CARSON "A.C." WALDREP

Before arriving at Loyola, Texas native Alfred Carson "A.C." Waldrep Jr. rounded up cattle and worked with his dad in the oilfields of Galveston Bay. He then attended Southwestern Louisiana Institute before going to Loyola for his graduate studies.

Waldrep became an oral and maxillofacial surgeon. He served twenty-two years in the military before joining the Medical University of South Carolina's College of Dental Medicine, where he was the assistant dean until his retirement on June 30, 1985. He also spent much of his time working with the Young Men's Christian Association (YMCA) in James Island, South Carolina.

Waldrep died in 2002 at age seventy-nine. He was married to his wife, Dorothy, for fifty-six years. They had three sons, one daughter and several grandchildren. He was buried in South Carolina.

THOMAS J. "T.J." WHITTAKER

Thomas J. "T.J." Whittaker had a good year in 1945. After his adventure in Kansas City in the spring with Loyola, he coached his alma mater Jesuit's American Legion baseball team to city, state and regional championships in the summer. He later played Minor League baseball in Trenton, New Jersey, and Springfield, Ohio, as well as semi-pro basketball for a team in New Orleans known as the Sports, his son Scott, remembers.

Whittaker's professional career ended after he badly injured his right shoulder and had to undergo surgery. Scott Whittaker said his dad subsequently made his living for a time working three jobs: delivering and picking up linens from restaurants, performing quality control for the local Falstaff brewery on Tulane Avenue and coaching at Stallings Playground near the New Orleans Fair Grounds until nine or ten o'clock most nights. "He was a hardworking guy, my dad was," Scott Whittaker said.

T.J. Whittaker met his future wife, Patricia, at Colonial Country Club one night in the late 1950s. Patricia, who was married and living in California at the time, had gone to the club to have dinner with her sister and brother-in-law, and T.J. was there, doing something that she loved very well. "He was a great dancer," she said. "And I loved to dance. So that's what we did."

As it turned out, Patricia ended up divorcing her husband, moving back to New Orleans, dating T.J. and then marrying him in 1959. Four years later, T.J. partnered with a man named Clendon J. Butera to open a school at 8400 Hayne Boulevard in New Orleans. Lake Castle Private School prided itself on providing an affordable, quality education to elementary students, and through the years, additional campuses in Slidell and Madisonville were founded. Patricia also worked at Lake Castle while her husband taught mathematics and directed the school's athletics program.

Though for a long while his wife had the miniature gold basketball her husband received in Kansas City in honor of the national championship, he never spoke much about what he accomplished with the Wolf Pack in 1945. "I didn't like basketball," said Patricia Whittaker, who noted the irony. "We only went to one basketball game that I can remember."

That might have been because the final game against Pepperdine wasn't an entirely pleasant experience for T.J. Whittaker. Scott Whittaker had the opportunity to speak with Coach Orsley one time at a ceremony honoring the '45 team at Loyola, and Orsley said that T.J. would've preferred to score many more than the three points he did in the title match. "The coach told me my dad did an outstanding job defensively, but he really wanted to score more," recalled Scott.

Regardless, at Lake Castle, Whittaker's involvement in sports continued. He coached the baseball team there, and "they won all kinds of awards," Patricia Whittaker said. According to Scott Whittaker, his dad "was very good at scouting the other teams and knowing their strengths and weaknesses and exploiting their weaknesses and protecting against their strengths. He was hard on his kids, but they loved him because they knew he cared."

T.J. Whittaker, who lived in Metairie for forty years, was planning to retire soon when he died of an apparent heart attack at home in 1991. He was sixty-four. He was buried in Greenwood Cemetery.

Aside from Scott, the Whittakers had another son, Grant. T.J. Whittaker also had a stepson, the late Jay R. Tingley, from Patricia Whittaker's previous marriage.

SAM CIOLINO

Sam Ciolino received his degree in dentistry in 1945. He subsequently served two years in the U.S. Navy, one of them treating patients while based in Seattle and another stationed in Yokohama, Japan. He launched his private practice in 1947 in Metairie, and he retired in 2013.

Competing and triumphing with the 1944–45 basketball team was "the biggest thrill," Ciolino said one afternoon at his office. "If it wasn't for the fact that a lot of guys were out at the war, I wouldn't have been on the team. I could see we had a lot of talent with them. I was glad to just be numbered with them." He also noted with a smile and a shake of the head, "Playing for Loyola just one year and winning it all was nice."

This page: Following his tenure at Loyola, Sam Ciolino served two years in the U.S. Navy and practiced dentistry until 2013. *Photos by Matthew Hinton.*

Ciolino has always been proud of what his teammates and coaches became following their moment of glory in Kansas City. "All of these guys went off to be successes. Never did I hear anything bad about any of them. They were good people." One of those men became his patient, too. Ciolino said he treated Jim Bonck for years.

Some New Orleanians will remember Ciolino from his involvement with the Knights of Columbus' Cardinal Gibbons Council 2918. He was the council's grand knight for a time.

Ciolino married Betty Kennedy Bonnecaze, who passed away on August 31, 2009. From her, he gained two stepchildren, Judith and Edward.

FRANK A. FRANCEVICH (FRANK FRANCE)

Frank A. Francevich, better known around New Orleans as Frank France, was the student manager for the 1944–45 Loyola Wolf Pack. However, he also played for the team sparingly and even netted a field goal in the December 17, 1944 game against Brookley. Though he didn't make much of a name for himself on Loyola's historic team, as an educator later in his life, he touched the lives of countless students in the metro New Orleans area.

France graduated from Loyola in 1949. That year, he co-founded a day camp with veteran educator Mary Patricia "Pat" Kehoe. They called it Kehoe-France, and it operated out of Audubon Park in its early days and various other rented facilities afterward.

France and Kehoe married in 1952. In 1956, Frank France received a master's degree in education from Loyola. Kehoe-France moved its campus permanently to 720 Elise Avenue in Metairie in 1958, and it has been there ever since. The day camp officially became a school in 1962, and in 1996, Kehoe-France opened a second campus at 25 Patricia Drive in Covington to serve the residents on the north shore of Lake Pontchartrain. More than 1,100 students attend the two campuses. The school's blue and white colors, as well as its genie lamp logo, are familiar sights on car bumper stickers in the area.

Frank France and his wife had four sons: Kevin, Michael, Kyle and Frank Jr. Pat Kehoe died of cancer at age sixty-six on May 19, 1995, and thirteen years later, Frank France experienced the loss of his son, Kevin. But there were happy days again for France after that.

In 2011, Loyola gave Frank France Sr. its highest honor, the Integritas Vitae Award. Recipients, the university says, display "high moral character and selfless service, without expectation of material reward or public recognition, and adhering to the principles of honesty, integrity, justice and the preservation of human dignity."

A past Integritas Vitae Award honoree was Mother Teresa, who was chosen the year she visited New Orleans. At the Integritas Vitae ceremony, France, who was eighty at the time, said, "I'm very honored and stunned at my age to be honored like this. I was exposed to some great people at Loyola, and it has remained with me all of my life."

He spoke literally. The octogenarian regularly attends Loyola's basketball games.

RAY LABORDE

Ray Laborde scored precisely 1 of the 1,569 points the Wolf Pack bucketed en route to the Maude A. Naismith national championship trophy in 1945. The walk-on—who lived at a boardinghouse for dental students adjacent to campus—made it on a free throw against Southwestern Louisiana Institute. Nonetheless, after graduation, he arguably attained greater fame in Louisiana than any other member of that team, as he became the right-hand man to a four-time Louisiana governor.

Raymond Julian Laborde was a high school freshman in Marksville, Louisiana, when he met classmate Edwin Washington Edwards in 1940. They took well to each other and became friends. Before long, the two ran against each other for class president. Laborde defeated Edwards, who would go on to become the only four-term governor in the history of Louisiana and one of only a few four-term governors ever in the country.

"Edwin said the girls voted for me, and that did it," Laborde said, chuckling. "We were too good of friends to let that come between us."

Laborde practiced sports after school, while Edwards worked a job. They spent time together as members of the marching band. "Edwin was very sharp in high school," Laborde remembered. "He pretty much corrected the teachers all of the time, that sort of thing."

Five years after they met, Ray Laborde moved to Uptown New Orleans, joined the Wolf Pack and was on the team that won New Orleans' only major basketball championship. In the meantime, Edwin Edwards, a student at LSU, "was on his way to the top in Baton Rouge," the capital of Louisiana, Laborde said.

The two friends kept in touch. Laborde served as mayor of Marksville for twelve years starting in 1958. He presided over the Louisiana Municipal Association in 1962. Voters from Avoyelles Parish then elected him to Louisiana's House of Representatives in 1972, where he served for twenty years. He served as the House speaker pro tempore from 1982 to 1984.

Meanwhile, Edwards won four gubernatorial terms—two terms from 1972 to 1980, one term from 1984 to 1988 and another from 1992 to 1996. During his last term, Edwards took his friend Ray to the top, appointing him as Louisiana's commissioner of administration, a position in which Laborde said he controlled every cent in the state's multimillion-dollar budget.

Many consider the commissioner of administration the second-most powerful man in Baton Rouge. "It was the crowning event of my life," Laborde said. He added, "Being able to call the shots was most satisfying." In 2003, Laborde earned enshrinement in the Louisiana Political Museum and Hall of Fame in Winnfield, Louisiana.

Sixty-one years after Ray Laborde and Edwin Edwards met, Edwards was sentenced to ten years in federal prison when then–U.S. Attorney Eddie Jordan and his assistant, Jim Letten (eventually the U.S. attorney for the Eastern District of Louisiana) convicted Edwards on seventeen charges of corruption, including extortion, mail fraud, racketeering and wire fraud. Three years after the former governor's imprisonment, his second marriage ended in divorce. But his friendship with Laborde held up. "Listen, I stick by my friends," said Laborde, who said he visited Edwards monthly at the federal prison in Oakdale, Louisiana. Edwards was released from prison in January 2011. He has since remarried.

Later in 2011, despite having recently undergone heart surgery, Laborde led the opposition to a plan by Louisiana governor Bobby Jindal to sell three state prisons to private groups. One of the prisons was in Avoyelles. Laborde criticized Jindal's administration for wanting to sell the Avoyelles facility for just $33 million when it was worth at least $50 million, simply to reduce the price the private group was going to charge Louisiana to oversee the prison. He pointed out that the Avoyelles prison provided jobs. Laborde then went to Baton Rouge, appeared in front of the state House Appropriations Committee and, according to the *Shreveport Times*, told them, "The governor, everywhere he goes, says this makes sense. I talked to some economists, and they said, 'Who in the hell came up with that idea?' My God, somebody's got to stop this runaway train. It's getting wilder every day."

Laborde's efforts paid off in the first round of that political battle, as the Appropriations Committee rejected Jindal's plan. In 2012, though, legislators decided to explore the possibility of hiring a private company to operate the Avoyelles prison while the state kept control of it. Critics said the change would jeopardize jobs.

Laborde minces no words when describing his role during Loyola's 1945 championship run. "I was like a sub's sub," he said. "It didn't get me any special treatment, being on the team, aside from maybe an extra pair of clean socks after practice. I was just honored to be on that team."

Today, Laborde owns the well-known Raymond's Department Store in Marksville at 317 North Main Street.

ASSISTANT COACH JAMES "BIG JIM" MCCAFFERTY

"Big Jim" McCafferty worked outside of the spotlight that Jack Orsley commanded for years. Players said he supplied a considerable portion of the brains behind Loyola's basketball operation. But at six-foot-eight, 280 pounds, he also supplied much of the brawn, standing a full four inches taller than center Joe Gurievsky, the 1944–45 team's tallest man.

"He was also a super dresser," Red Hultberg remembers. "He always said, 'It doesn't cost much more to go first class.' Always well-groomed, well-dressed." Marion Hultberg, a cheerleader sensitive to those types of things in 1945, agreed. "A very, very nice-looking man," she judged, nodding for emphasis.

McCafferty was born a nineteen-pound baby in Scammon, Kansas, to Irish immigrants. He moved to Henryetta, Oklahoma, and unsurprisingly became a high-school basketball star. He went to college one year in Kansas before working at a steel mill in Henryetta and roughnecking with a drilling crew in Oklahoma oil fields. In 1938, McCafferty accepted a football scholarship to Loyola University in New Orleans. As a sophomore, he lettered. The university retired the football program in 1939, but McCafferty remained loyal to the Wolf Pack and shone in basketball during his last three years.

As a senior captain in 1942, McCafferty helped the Jack Orsley–coached Wolf Pack win the Dixie Conference championship and earned Most Valuable Player honors. He graduated from Loyola with a BS in physical education. After being hired at his alma mater as assistant athletic director, he coached track for eleven years and was the assistant basketball coach for eight years. McCafferty became Loyola's head basketball coach when the school competed in the NCAA, taking the Wolf Pack to NCAA tournament appearances in 1954 and 1957.

Though he was an assistant to Coach Orsley, brawny Jim McCafferty supplied much of the brains that fueled Loyola's basketball team, according to players. *Courtesy Loyola University New Orleans Athletics Hall of Fame.*

His accomplishments away from Loyola's campus also help illustrate his mastery of coaching the game of basketball. In 1948, United States of America Basketball entrusted him with coaching a team of collegiate all-stars at the Central American Olympic Games in Panama. McCafferty delivered—his team won a gold medal. In 1957, after his last appearance with Loyola at the NCAA tournament, fellow Jesuit school Xavier University in Cincinnati offered him the job of head basketball coach. He accepted, leaving Loyola.

In some photos, McCafferty's face resembles that of actor Kyle Chandler, who portrayed Coach Eric Taylor on the television show *Friday Night Lights.* A Hollywood-ready coach when it came to looks, upon taking the Xavier job, McCafferty produced a Hollywood-worthy season with his basketball team.

On the way to its National Invitational Tournament bid in 1958, McCafferty coached Xavier to a number-four ranking in the United Press International poll and a number-seven ranking in the Associated Press poll. McCafferty and the Musketeers then won the NIT championship at Madison Square Garden in New York City. *Sport* magazine called it "one of the greatest upsets in basketball history."

McCafferty's ninety-one-win mark was third best at Xavier when he died in 2006. He had coached seven one-thousand-point scorers and had taken Xavier to its first NCAA tournament in 1961. McCafferty retired as head coach in 1963 but served as the university's athletic director until 1979.

In 1979, McCafferty became the first commissioner of what is today the Horizon League, an NCAA conference. Nowadays, whichever Horizon League school collects the most points awarded for accomplishments in athletics each year wins the James J. McCafferty Trophy.

McCafferty was ninety when he died in Seattle. The McCafferty family said that "Big Jim" never forgot his days as student, player and coach at Loyola, and after his death, they asked that, in lieu of flowers, people make donations in his name to the Wolf Pack athletic department. McCafferty is enshrined in the Loyola Athletics Hall of Fame, the Xavier Athletics Hall of Fame and the Allstate Sugar Bowl Greater New Orleans Sports Hall of Fame.

COACH JOHN C. "JACK" ORSLEY

Jack Orsley's 173 wins from 1940 to 1949 make a career mark that sixteen other coaches heading Loyola's basketball program have not come close to equaling for decades. Orsley also oversaw four seasons of 20 or more wins from 1943 to 1948, and he is the only Loyola basketball coach to accomplish that. In fact, only one other men's basketball coach at Loyola has eclipsed the 100-win mark; Michael Giorlando reached that total in 2012.

John C. Orsley was born in 1905 in Port Allegany, Pennsylvania, and grew up in Elmira Heights, New York. In 1928, he graduated from the University of Illinois and went on to earn a master's degree in educational administration from Columbia University. He coached baseball and basketball for forty-five years in New Orleans, starting at Isidore Newman School from 1928 to 1933. He went to Jesuit High from 1933 to 1936 and returned to Newman from 1936 to 1940. He then worked for seventeen years at Loyola, where he also coached some of the university's most accomplished baseball teams. His final coaching jobs were at East Jefferson High School from 1957 to 1959 and Tulane University from 1959 to 1973.

For the record, neither Jack Atchley nor Jim Hultberg thought Orsley possessed unusual basketball knowledge. In their opinion, Loyola's most successful basketball coach "wasn't the greatest basketball coach in the world," as Jim Hultberg muttered one day in 2007. "Tons and tons of talent" was the reason Orsley and the university won their only national championship, Hultberg opined. And, Atchley added, it was Orsley's ability to organize that talent—with a considerable helping hand from Jim McCafferty—that enabled Loyola to make history in 1945.

Coach Orsley "was a very good organizer," Atchley said. "He was a great organizer." Orsley had enough sense to simply augment the savvy court leadership of Foreman and Casteix with the raw talents of Whittaker, Hultberg, Gurievsky and Chollet. He organized his system around the parts given to him rather than trying to jam parts such as Whittaker, Hultberg, Gurievsky and Chollet into a pre-built system.

Perhaps Orsley's best asset was his boiling competitiveness. Jack Atchley served up an example. On a day off from practice during the 1944–45 season, Atchley was enjoying a walk around Loyola's campus. Suddenly, he bumped into Orsley, who was carrying a tennis racket and headed toward the gym.

"Hey, Jack," Orsley greeted his freshman forward. "Do you want to come play some tennis with me?"

Atchley had never played, but ignorant of the sport's complexities, he figured, "It can't be that hard. It's just running from side to side and hitting a ball over the net."

Orsley woefully overpowered Atchley during their match. He whipped his freshman charge in straight sets, mercilessly hammering shot after shot by him. "I learned some things about tennis that day from Coach," Atchley remembers, his laugh uncontrollable. "They were, 'Don't play' and 'Coach did not like to lose.'"

In addition, Orsley intensely disliked unfitness. At a university convocation following the national championship, he addressed students and faculty on the importance of maintaining and even expanding the physical education component in the curriculum. He suggested that the United States was paying in lives and money for the poor shape many young men fighting in World War II were in. "If America had a physical education program before the war, many of the boys who made the supreme sacrifice would be alive today, and [their] fathers would not have to be drafted," he said.

In other ways, though, Orsley was benevolent with his players. "He gave me a ride home after practice every night," said Hultberg, who otherwise would have had to walk about six miles to get to his home in the Lakeview section of New Orleans. "Can you imagine if I had to walk that?"

During a 1989 interview with the *Times-Picayune*, Orsley said he was particularly proud of the fact that his team achieved the championship with practically no recruiting budget. "Our entire athletic budget was around $50,000," he told the newspaper.

Orsley was inducted into Loyola's Athletics Hall of Fame in 1967. He spent his later years landscaping and fishing in a lake behind a large property he owned in Carriere, Mississippi, according to the *Times-Picayune* article. Orsley died in 1996 at age ninety-one at a hospital in Picayune, Mississippi. He was laid to rest at Metairie Cemetery.

Leroy Chollet

In February 1998, Leroy Chollet was honored for his service at St. Edward High School, the only place he coached and taught. He died in June of that year at seventy-three due to complications from Lou Gehrig's disease, which his brother also had. Leroy Chollet rests at Milan Cemetery in Milan, Ohio. He left behind two sons—Lawrence of Nyack, New York, and David—and a daughter, Melanie Lynch of Lakewood, Ohio.

Kluck's Restaurant, the seafood joint and Lakewood landmark where Chollet was a bartender, closed in 2007, according to news reports in the *Cleveland Plain Dealer*.

Meanwhile, there is a poster-sized black-and-white portrait photo of the 1945 national champions that has hung in various rooms on Loyola's campus.

As a result of water damage, one player's face on the picture has faded off. That face is Leroy Chollet's.

The Loyola Wolf Pack Basketball Program

After Leroy Chollet and his family left New Orleans, Loyola basketball never again repeated the glories of the 1944–45 season. In 1945–46, Jack Orsley coached the Wolf Pack to the NAIB tournament semifinals, but they lost in that round by sixteen points.

In the 1950s, Loyola played in the NCAA and qualified for that organization's national tournament in 1954, 1957 and 1958. The Wolf Pack had the worst luck any small school in those single-elimination competitions could have. Each time, in the opening round, they played as the away team, either in their opponent's home city or very close to it. At its first NCAA appearance, under the direction of Orsley's former assistant Jim McCafferty, Loyola lost to Notre Dame in Fort Wayne, Indiana.

Still coached by McCafferty, the Wolf Pack then dropped its second NCAA outing to Oklahoma City University in Oklahoma City. And, in the first game of Loyola's last trip to the NCAA tournament, Loyola—coached by Jim Harding in those days—lost to Oklahoma State University on that school's home floor in Stillwater, Oklahoma. Oklahoma State in those days was led by coaching legend Hank Iba, who guided that team to NCAA titles in 1945 and 1946. Iba is also remembered for coaching United States basketball teams to Olympic gold medals in 1964 in Tokyo and 1968 in Mexico City, and to a controversial silver medal in 1972 in Munich.

The years following the NCAA appearances for Loyola were pretty sparse. The program's only winning seasons came in 1970–71 and 1971–72, when Loyola finished 16–10 and 14–11, respectively. Then, in the spring of 1972, the university called a press conference and announced that it was disbanding its entire intercollegiate athletics program. School officials said they made the decision to save money and prioritize education.

Loyola wouldn't reinstitute varsity sports on campus until the 1991–92 basketball season. The new Wolf Pack men's basketball team was coached by Jerry Hernandez, and it competed in the National Association of Intercollegiate Athletics, the NAIB's successor. At its inception, the new program was not able to offer athletic scholarships and was not funded by the university. Loyola didn't win a game until the third outing of its second season.

But in the fourth year of varsity sports' resurrection at Loyola, the men's basketball team went 7–1 in its region and won the regular-season title. Loyola then won the regional tournament and earned an invitation to a national meet for the first time since Oklahoma State bounced the Maroon-and-Gold from the NCAA field in 1958. In 2012, under coach Michael

Giorlando, Loyola won twenty games for the first time since Orsley's tenure. It also secured a conference division title.

Meanwhile, the Loyola women's basketball team returned the Wolf Pack to brilliance from 2006 to 2009. Under coach DoBee Plaisance, Loyola won regular-season conference titles in 2007 and 2008, and a conference tournament title in 2007. In 2009, under the direction of coach Kellie Kennedy, Loyola again won the regular-season conference and conference tournament championships. Each year in this time period, Loyola's women's basketball team earned berths in the national tournament, and in 2008 it advanced to the quarterfinals, or the Elite Eight round.

The Wolf Pack's success was in large part due to twin sisters Trenese and Trenell Smith. Trenese was the first Loyola basketball player to break the 2,000-point barrier and was the school's all-time career scoring leader when her time at the university was done. She was a two-time All-American, three-

Members of the 1944–45 Loyola Wolf Pack. *From left to right*: Sam Ciolino, Ray Laborde, Jack Atchley, Sam Foreman, John Casteix, Tommy Whittaker, Jim Hultberg, Leroy Chollet, A.C. Waldrep, Jim Bonck, Warren Willkomm and Joe Gurievsky. *Courtesy of Scott Whittaker.*

time conference Player of the Year and was ranked as one of the four best female college athletes of the decade in 2010 by the *Times-Picayune*. Trenell, meanwhile, was a two-time All-American honorable mention and finished her career third in all-time scoring with more than 1,700 points.

Indeed, there have been triumphant basketball teams at Loyola through the years since March 1945. The Smith sisters were two of the best athletes ever to represent Loyola, and Trenese, to many, is the most successful figure in the modern era of athletics at the university. But no Wolf Pack basketball player has ever been able to challenge all of the achievements Leroy Chollet had in one brilliant season on the campus, which today is bordered by Freret Street, St. Charles Avenue, Calhoun Street and West Road.

There is no telling how far Leroy Chollet could have taken Loyola, if not all of New Orleans, in his sophomore, junior and senior seasons. But New Orleans didn't wait to find out, because Leroy Chollet's family was part black—and regrettably, shamefully, maddeningly, in this city, in those days, that was unacceptable.

Appendix I

Summary of Results

1944–45 Loyola University Wolf Pack
Coach: Jack Orsley
Record: 25–5

Regular Season

Opponent	Result
Big Spring AAF	W, 59–38
Bergstrom AAF	L, 55–61
Bergstrom AAF	W, 54–42
New Orleans Naval AS	W, 37–29
Brookley AAF	W, 65–38
Naval Repair Base	W, 65–52
U.S. Coast Guard	W, 53–26
Foster General Hospital	W, 52–50
Gulfport AAF	W, 51–50
Millsaps	W, 53–36
Lake Charles AAF	W, 73–53
Keesler Field	L, 39–42

Opponent	Result
Keesler Field	W, 52–45
Southwestern La.	W, 62–47
Gulfport NTC	W, 48–47
Jackson Barracks	L, 47–48
Coast Guard RS	W, 77–43
Jackson Barracks	W, 38–25
Eighth Naval District	W, 52–50
Southwestern La.	W, 55–48
Naval Repair Base	W, 63–52
Millsaps	W, 49–47
Foster General Hospital	L, 41–51
Camp Plauche 46	W, 60–46
Gulfport NTC 70	L, 46–70
Camp Plauche	W, 73–41

National Championship Tournament, Kansas City

Phillips University	First Round	W, 53–31
Central Normal	Quarterfinals	W, 60–46
Southern Illinois	Semifinals	W, 37–35
Pepperdine	Finals	W, 49–36

Appendix II

Loyola University Wolf Pack

1944-45 Roster

Regular Season Roster

Coach: Jack Orsley
Assistant Coach: Jim McCafferty

Players:

Bill Browning
Jim Bonck
Freddie Chaplain
Joe Gurievsky
A.C. Waldrep
Leroy Chollet
Sam Foreman (co-captain)
Jim Hultberg
Warren Willkomm
John Casteix (co-captain)
Tommy Whittaker
Sam Ciolino
Frank Francevich
Don Mahoney
Ray Laborde

Jack Atchley
Sal Sunseri

Student Manager: Frank Francevich

1945 National Tournament Roster

Starters:

Tommy Whittaker
Jim Hultberg
Johnny Casteix
Leroy Chollet
Jim Bonck

Bench:

Joe Gurievsky
Sam Ciolino
A.C. Waldrep
Jack Atchley

Individual Scoring Totals

Regular Season

Player	FG	FT	Total Points
Leroy Chollet	132	62	326
Jim Hultberg	116	46	278
T.J. Whittaker	112	11	235
Sam Foreman	92	42	226
Joe Gurievsky	40	31	111
John Casteix	32	25	89
Jim Bonck	25	4	54
A.C. Waldrep	15	7	37
Fred Chaplain	13	5	31

Player	FG	FT	Total Points
Bill Browning	4	4	12
Sam Ciolino	3	2	8
Jack Atchley	3	1	7
F. Francevich	1	0	2
Don Mahoney	1	0	2
Ray Laborde	0	1	1

Tournament Totals

Player	FG	FT	Total Points
Leroy Chollet	24	13	61
Jim Bonck	18	4	40
Jim Hultberg	15	6	36
John Casteix	13	5	31
T.J. Whittaker	8	3	19
Joe Gurievsky	4	1	9
A.C. Waldrep	1	1	3
Sam Ciolino	0	0	0
Jack Atchley	0	0	0

Season Totals

Player	FG	FT	Total Points
Leroy Chollet	156	75	387
Jim Hultberg	131	52	314
T.J. Whittaker	120	14	254
Sam Foreman	92	42	226
John Casteix	45	30	120
Joe Gurievsky	44	32	120

Player	FG	FT	Total Points
Jim Bonck	43	8	94
A.C. Waldrep	16	8	40
Fred Chaplain	13	5	31
Bill Browning	4	4	12
Sam Ciolino	3	2	8
Jack Atchley	3	1	7
F. Francevich	1	0	2
Don Mahoney	1	0	2
Ray Laborde	0	1	1

Works Consulted

Chapter 1

Finney, Peter. "Flashback/Sammy Trombatore." *Times-Picayune*, February 19, 1984, Section 6, 8.

"Four 100-point Men on Pack." *Times-Picayune*, February 18, 1944, 13.

"Loyola Accepts Invitation to National Cage Tourney." *The Maroon*, March 2, 1945, 3.

"Loyola Declines Invitation to Play in National Meet." *Times-Picayune*, February 25, 1943, 15.

"McCafferty's Late Scoring Beats Spring Hill for Loyola, Gives Pack Title." *Times-Picayune*, March 5, 1942, 16.

Miller, Madeline. "From Camp to Campus: Ed Fricke Is First Former Staffer Wounded in Action." *The Maroon*, April 6, 1944, 2.

———. "From Camp to Campus: Lt. Perret Now Wears Two Battle Stars and Air Medal." *The Maroon*, April 20, 1945, 2.

———. "From Camp to Campus: Once Maroon Sports Editor, He Now Sports Shining Bars." *The Maroon*, April 13, 1945, 2.

"Trombatore to Army," *Times-Picayune*, April 11, 1944, 13.

Zollinger, Marjorie. "Loyola to Pay Tribute to 30 Who Died in War." *The Maroon*, November 3, 1944, 1.

Chapter 2

Comar, Emile. "Ask Big Joe How to Become a Track Star in One Season." *The Maroon*, March 16, 1945, 3.

———. "Red Is Second to None in All-Around Play." *The Maroon*, February 23, 1945, 3.

———. "Top Scorer on Cage Team, Chollet Is All-Around Athlete." *The Maroon*, February 16, 1945, 3.

———. "Whittaker Can Claim Title of All-Around Sports Star." *The Maroon*, March 2, 1945, 3.

Ducote, Kirby. "Pitchouts: Loyola University's Ancient But Historic Gym." *Times-Picayune*, April 27, 1953, 27.

"Four 100-point Men on Pack," *Times-Picayune*, February 18, 1944, 13.

Louisiana's Ragin' Cajuns Athletics Network. "Spotlight on Former Athlete: Dr. Sam Foreman." http://www.athleticnetwork.net/site.php?pageID=55&profID=152.

"Loyola Bows to Bergstrom." *Times-Picayune*, December 9, 1944, 8.

"Loyola Quint vs. Bergstrom." *Times-Picayune*, December 7, 1944, 18.

Chapter 3

Keefe, Wm. McG. "Viewing the News: Coaching Made Loyola." *Times-Picayune*, March 19, 1945, 10.

"Key Club's Teen Canteen Is Open." *Times-Picayune*, May 27, 1944, 12.

"Lieut. Rau Receives Medal For Gallantry in Action." *The Maroon*, April 27, 1945, 3.

"Loyola to Meet Naval Air Team in Basketball Tonight." *Times-Picayune*, December 14, 1944, 22.

"Loyola Wins Over Flyers." *Times-Picayune*, December 10, 1944, 29.

"Loyola Wins Over Flyers." *Times-Picayune*, December 15, 1944, 15.

Miller, Madeline. "From Camp to Campus: Ed Fricke Is First Former Staffer Wounded in Action," *The Maroon*, April 6, 1945, 2.

———. "From Camp to Campus: Former Loyolan Sees World by Piloting His Own Ship." *The Maroon*, February 16, 1945, 2.

———. "From Camp to Campus: Loyolans in France Revel in Glories of Gay Paree." *The Maroon*, March 23, 1945, 2.

———. "From Camp to Campus: Prisoner's Morale High, Expects to be Back Soon." *The Maroon*, February 9, 1945, 2.

Mumme, Jeannette. "Movies Plus Lenfant's Equals One Good Date, Loyolans Say." *The Maroon*, February 2, 1945, 1.

Schneider, Frank. "Lenfant's Legacy Full of Memories." *Times-Picayune*, August 16, 1990, E1.

"Wolves Beat Coast Guard." *Times-Picayune*, December 23, 1944, 9.

"Wolves Beat Flyers, Sailors, As Chollet Scores 50 Points." *The Maroon*, December 22, 1944, 3.

Chapter 4

Alexander, James R. "Foreman, Whittaker Lead Loyola to 52–36 Win Over Millsaps." *Times-Picayune*, January 10, 1945, 10.

———. "Keesler Field Stops Loyola Winning Streak with 42–39 Victory." *Times-Picayune*, January 14, 1945, 20.

———. "Loyola Edges Past Gulfport Navy Quint, 48–47, in Hard-Fought Tilt Before Packed Gym." *Times-Picayune*, January 24, 1945, 9.

———. "Loyola Goes Wild in 2nd Half to Trounce Lake Charles, 73–53," *Times-Picayune*, January 13, 1945, 10.

———. "Loyola Rallies to Beat Keesler, 52–45," *Times-Picayune*, January 20, 1945, 8.

———. "Loyola Seeks Revenge in Return Game with Keesler Tonight." *Times-Picayune*, January 19, 1945, 12.

Keefe, Wm. McG. "Viewing the News: That Big Gym Again." *Times-Picayune*, January 24, 1945, 8.

"Loyola Bows to Barracks." *Times-Picayune*, January 28, 1945, 23.

"Loyola Faces Tough Quintet from Keesler Field Friday." *Times-Picayune*, January 18, 1945,14.

"Loyola Scores 62–47 Victory Over S.L.I. Bulldogs at Lafayette." *Times-Picayune*, January 21, 1945, 21.

"Loyola Will Play Strong Gulfport Flyers in Basketball Contest This Afternoon." *Times-Picayune*, January 7, 1945, 19.

McDonnell, Bill. "Wolves to Battle Undefeated Keesler Quintet This Week." *The Maroon*, January 12, 1945, 3.

"Wolves Win Thriller to Run String to Five." *The Maroon*, January 12, 1945, 3.

Chapter 5

Alexander, James R. "Loyola Cagers Defeat Camp Plauche Handily, 60–46, for 20th Victory of Season." *Times-Picayune*, February 22, 1945, 11.

———. "Loyola Quintet Overwhelms Coast Guard Team, 77 to 43." *Times-Picayune*, February 2, 1945, 10.

———. "Loyola Trims Navy R. Base." *Times-Picayune*, February 14, 1945, 15.

———. "S.L.I. Bulldogs Extend Loyola Wolves But Bow to Superior Pack in Close Game." *Times-Picayune*, February 11, 1945, 23.

———. "Wolves Prep for Plauche." *Times-Picayune*, February 20, 1945, 9.

Brown, Gernon Jr. "Wolves' Close Shaves Give Heart Diseases to Followers." *The Maroon*, February 16, 1945, 3.

———. "Wolves Didn't Need Football Tactics to Defeat Barracks." *The Maroon*, February 9, 1945, 3.

"Gulfport Whips Loyola Quintet." *Times-Picayune*, February 26, 1945, 10.

Hart, Carol. "Loyola Beats Barracks, 38 to 25," *Times-Picayune*, February 4, 1945, 23.

Lousteau, A.J. "Pack Beats Plauche, Splits Road Games." *The Maroon*, February 23, 1945, 3.

"Loyola Accepts Invitation to National Cage Tourney." *The Maroon*, March 2, 1945, 3.

"Loyola Five Bows to Foster Quint." *Times-Picayune*, February 19, 1945, 10.

"Loyola Wins Over Millsaps." *Times-Picayune*, February 17, 1945, 9.

"Loyola Wolves Eke Out Close Win Over Navy Team." *Times-Picayune*, February 10, 1945, 9.

"L.S.U. Defeats Northwestern '5,'" *Times-Picayune*, February 24, 1945, 8.

Mumme, Jeannette. "Terror Bombing of Germany Uncalled For, Loyolans Say." *The Maroon*, March 2, 1945, 1.

"Pack Ends Season with 21 Victories." *The Maroon*, March 2, 1945, 3.

Phillips, Billy. "Loyola Wolves Easily Beat Camp Plauche Quint, 73–41," *Times-Picayune*, March 1, 1945, 16.

"Wolves Will Play Gulfport, Plauche, May Play in National Meet." *The Maroon*, February 23, 1945, 3.

CHAPTER 6

Ballparks.com. "Municipal Auditorium." http://basketball.ballparks.com/NBA/KansasCityKings/oldindex.htm.

"Banquet Held for Wolves, Coaches." *The Maroon*, April 13, 1945, 3.

Brown, Gernon Jr. "Coach Orsley Made Champs Out of Freshman Cagers." *The Maroon*, April 6, 1945, 3.

"Cheney Defeated at Kansas City." *Ellensburg Daily Record*, March 14, 1945, 8.

Finney, Peter. "Anniversary Sees New Title Dreams." *Times-Picayune*, February 17, 1995, D1.

Hart, Carol. "Loyola's Cage Champs Called Greatest Wolfpack Team Ever." *Times-Picayune*, April 11, 1945, 10.

———. "Loyola's Champions Greeted by Noisy Celebration Upon Return." *Times-Picayune*, March 20, 1945, 10.

Keefe, Wm. McG. "Viewing the News: Coaching Made Loyola." *Times-Picayune*, March 19, 1945, 10.

"Loyola Beats Pepperdine, 49–36, for National Basket Crown." *Times-Picayune*, March 19, 1945,10.

"Loyola Beats Phillips University, 53–31, in College Tourney." *Times-Picayune*, March 15, 1945, 19.

"Loyola Squad of Nine to Leave for Kansas City." *Times-Picayune*, March 10, 1945, 9.

"Loyola Wins in Last Minute, 37–35, to Reach Tourney Finals." *Times-Picayune*, March 17, 1945, 7.

"Loyola Wins National Intercollegiate Basketball Title." *The Maroon*, March 23, 1945, 3.

"Loyola Wolves Win Way into Kansas City Tourney Semifinals." *Times-Picayune*, March 16, 1945, 13.

Mouledoux, Elaine. "Come to the Victory Dance; Help Congratulate the Team." *The Maroon*, April 6, 1945, 4.

Roesler, Bob. "Behind the Sports Scene: Remembering the Wolfpack." *Times-Picayune*, April 2, 1972, Section 6, 2.

"Teams Arriving for College Play." *Times-Picayune*, March 13, 1945, 12.

"Wolfpack Defeat Phillips 53–31 in National Basketball Tourney." *The Maroon*, March 16, 1945, 3.

Chapter 7

Baranick, Alana. "Leroy Chollet, St. Ed's Teacher, Coach." *Cleveland Plain Dealer*, June 14, 1998, Metro, 6B.

Benjamin, Jack. "Holy Cross Beats Jesuit for State and City Cage Title." *Times-Picayune*, March 11, 1945, 21.

Bernstein, Mark F. *Football: The Ivy League Origins of an American Obsession*. Philadelphia: University of Pennsylvania Press, 2001: 189–90.

Brennan, Charles. "Holy Cross Wins State Crown by Beating Baton Rouge, 39–24." *Times-Picayune*, March 14, 1943, 22.

Chollet, Michael. "Descendants of Louis Philippe Chollet." http://familytreemaker.genealogy.com/users/c/h/o/Michael-G-Chollet/GENE5-0002.html.

———. "Descendants of Louis Philippe Chollet: Generation No. 4." http://familytreemaker.genealogy.com/users/c/h/o/Michael-G-Chollet/GENE5-0005.html.

———. "The Chollet Family." http://familytreemaker.genealogy.com/users/c/h/o/Michael-G-Chollet/index.html.

Cornell University Athletics. "(Basketball) Statistics Summary for 1947–1948." http://www.cornellbigred.com/documents/2008/6/17/1947_48.pdf?id=1123.

———. "(Football) Statistics Summary for 1948." http://www.cornellbigred.com/documents/2010/6/9/FB_1948.pdf?id=3018.

———. "(Football) Statistics Summary for 1949." http://www.cornellbigred.com/documents/2010/6/9/FB_1949.pdf?id=3018.

———. "Hall of Fame: Hillary A. Chollet, Class of 1949." http://www.cornellbigred.com/hof.aspx?hof=6&path=&kiosk.

Hannum, Alex, and Frank Deford. "Old Days and Changed Ways." *Sports Illustrated*, November 25, 1968. http://sportsillustrated.cnn.com/vault/article/magazine/MAG1148049/index.htm.

Hart, Carol. "Holy Cross Power Crushes Nicholls in CYO Grid Classic, 46–0." *Times-Picayune*, December 18, 1944, 14.

Keefe, Wm. McG. "Viewing the News: Chollet at Tulane." *Times-Picayune*, July 13, 1945, 10.

"Leroy P. Chollet, Canisius College Basketball Great." *Buffalo News*, June 16, 1998, Local, 1E.

Loyola University New Orleans Wolf Pack Hall of Fame. "Charles Powell (1967–69)." http://wolfpack.loyno.edu/wolfpack-hall-fame#powell.

"LSU Bows to Canisius." *Times-Picayune*, December 15, 1947, 23.

Maxse, Joe. "NBA's Early Days Gone But Not Forgotten: Ex-Player Recalls First Championship Series." *Cleveland Plain Dealer*, June 1, 1993, Sports, 2F.

"Milestones: A Century of Loyola History." http://www.loyno.edu/2012/milestones.

Opotowsky, Stanford. "Chollet Boys Steal Show as Holy Cross Captures First State Cage Crown." *Times-Picayune*, March 16, 1942, 14.

Thamel, Pete. "Grier Integrated a Game and Earned the World's Respect." *New York Times*, January 1, 2006.

"Tiger Cagers Taste Defeat." *Times-Picayune*, December 23, 1946, 14.

Vintage Basketball Autographs. "Hoop Stars of the Past—1920s through 1960s." http://www.freewebs.com/vintagebasketballautographs/forwards.htm.

Weinstein, Jeffrey. "'Hula Lou' Left Lasting Impact." *The Heights*, February 2, 2006. http://www.bcheights.com/2.6175/hula-lou-left-lasting-impact-1.913900.

Chapter 8

Allstate Sugar Bowl Greater New Orleans Sports Hall of Fame. "Jim McCafferty." http://www.allstatesugarbowl.org/site455.php.

Allstate Sugar Bowl Greater New Orleans Sports Hall of Fame, "Johnny Altobello," accessed April 7, 2013, http://www.allstatesugarbowl.org/site123.php.

Antunovich, Jack. "Jesuit Qualifies for Sectionals by Swamping Oklahoma, 12–1." *Times-Picayune*, August 18, 1945, 9.

Baranick, Alana. "Leroy Chollet, St. Ed's Teacher, Coach." *Cleveland Plain Dealer*, June 14, 1998, Metro, 6B.

"Casteix Seeks 7th Ward Post." *Times-Picayune*, January 21, 1966, Section 3, 2.

Comar, Emile. "Ask Big Joe How to Become a Track Star in One Season." *The Maroon*, March 16, 1945, 3.

"Dr. Ciolino Heads KC Council 2918." *Times-Picayune*, July 11, 1953, 5.

Dwyer, Eddie. "Maple Height Drops Bedford into GCC Tie." *Cleveland Plain Dealer*, February 26, 1998, Sports, 7D.

"Ex-Jesuit, Loyola Standout Dies." *Times-Picayune*, June 7, 2000, Sports, D9.

Finney, Peter. "Flashback/Sammy Trombatore." *Times-Picayune*, February 19, 1984, Section 6, 8.

"Frederick Louis Chaplain Sr." *Times-Picayune*, August 19, 1994, B4.

"Funeral Notice; Ciolino." *Times-Picayune*, September 3, 2009, Metro, B5.

"Funeral Notice; Hultberg," *Times-Picayune*, September 20, 2012, Metro.

Galuszka, Garrett. "Loyola Men's Basketball Wins SSAC West Title." *The Maroon*, March 1, 2012. http://www.loyolamaroon.com/2.6712/loyola-men-s-basketball-wins-ssac-west-title-1.2709491#.UWIv8hyiu68.

Hasten, Mike. "Panel Blocks Sale of Prisons." *Shreveport Times*, June 7, 2011.

The Jordy Hultberg Show. "Bio." http://thejordyhultbergshow.com/bio/.

Louisiana's Ragin' Cajuns Athletics Network. "Spotlight on Former Athlete: Dr. Sam Foreman." http://www.athleticnetwork.net/site.php?pageID=55&profID=152.

"Loyola Honors 72 Students." *The Maroon*, April 6, 1945, 4.

Loyola University New Orleans. *2009–2010 Men's Basketball Media Guide.*

———. *2009–2010 Women's Basketball Media Guide.*

———. "France Honored with Integritas Vitae Award Last Night." March 18, 2011. http://www.loyno.edu/news/laag/20110318/2772.

———. "Trenese Smith Listed among The Times-Picayune's Female College Athletes of the Decade." January 15, 2010.

Loyola University New Orleans Wolf Pack Hall of Fame. "'Big' Jim McCafferty (1938–1957)." http://wolfpack.loyno.edu/wolfpack-hall-fame#McCafferty.

Lubinger, Bill. "Landmark Kluck's Closing Friday." *Cleveland Plain Dealer*, September 5, 2007, Arts & Life, E8.

"Mary Patricia Kehoe France." *Times-Picayune*, May 21, 1995, Metro, B4.

Meyerson, Ernie. "Six Champions Crowned in Novice Boxing Tournament." *Times-Picayune*, March 24, 1943, 13.

"Milestones: A Century of Loyola History." http://www.loyno.edu/2012/milestones.

Millhollon, Michelle. "Jindal Backs Down from Sale of Prison." *Baton Rouge Advocate*, April 19, 2012, A4.

———. "Prison Plan Dominates Public Comment Session." *Baton Rouge Advocate*, April 8, 2011, A1.

"Retired Coach and Teacher Jack Orsley Is Dead at 91." *Times-Picayune*, April 23, 1996, B4.

Roesler, Bob. "Behind the Sports Scene: Remembering the Wolfpack." *Times-Picayune*, April 2, 1972, Section 6, 2.

Sports Reference LLC. "Oklahoma City vs. Loyola (LA) Box Score, March 12, 1957." http://www.sports-reference.com/cbb/boxscores/1957-03-12-loyola-la.html.

Sports Reference LLC. "Oklahoma State vs. Loyola (LA) Box Score, March 11, 1958." http://www.sports-reference.com/cbb/boxscores/1958-03-11-loyola-la.html.

Tributes.com. "Dr. Alfred Carson Waldrep, Jr." http://www.tributes.com/show/Alfred-Carson-Waldrep-56636255.

"Trombatore—Samuel Trombatore." *Times-Picayune*, July 28, 1991.

"Vote Certified in House Races." *Times-Picayune*, February 18, 1966, Section 3, 6.

"Whittaker—T.J. Whittaker Jr." *Times-Picayune*, June 17, 199.

Xavier Athletics. "James J. McCafferty." http://www.goxavier.com/genrel/mccafferty_jamesj00.html.

Index

D

E

F

G

H

J

K

L

M

N

About the Author

Ramon Antonio Vargas was a former editor and sportswriter for *The Maroon*, Loyola University New Orleans' campus newspaper. He is a staff writer for the *Times-Picayune* and NOLA.com, and his work has won numerous awards from organizations such as the Louisiana Press Association, the Press Club of New Orleans and Associated Press Media Editors. Born in 1986 and raised in the New Orleans suburb of Metairie, Vargas attended Stuart Hall School, Jesuit High School and Loyola. At Loyola, he developed a fascination with the university's storied athletic history, which he wrote numerous articles about for *The Maroon* and ultimately inspired him to author this book.

www.ingramcontent.com/pod-product-compliance
Lightning Source LLC
LaVergne TN
LVHW010949100826
845153LV00002B/177
9781540232960